LOVE'S FUGUE

Love's Fugue

Translation and Commentary on 'The Finest Song of All'

Mother
Xavier McMonagle, OSB

Hodder & Stoughton
LONDON SYDNEY AUCKLAND

First published in Great Britain in 1995 by Hodder and Stoughton
A division of Hodder Headline PLC

British Library Cataloguing in Publication Data

A record for this book is available
from the British Library

ISBN 0 340 63045 0

Typeset by Hewer Text Composition Services, Edinburgh
Printed and bound in Great Britain by
Cox & Wyman Ltd, Reading, Berks.

Hodder and Stoughton
A division of Hodder Headline PLC
338 Euston Road
London NW1 3BH

Contents

Acknowledgements

The author owes an inestimable debt of gratitude to the following persons who have advised and commented on the text during its writing and evolution:

Rabbi Lionel Blue, MA.

Revd Dom Jean Leclercq, OSB, Clervaux Abbaye, Luxembourg.

Rabbi Jonathan Magonet, MB, BS, PhD, Principal of the Leo Baeck College, and the Sternberg Centre for Judaism, London.

Revd Dom Daniel Rees, OSB, MA, STL, LSS, Downside Abbey, Master of Studies for the English Benedictine Congregation.

Rt Revd Dom Patrick Barry, OSB, MA, Abbot of Ampleforth.

Teresa de Bertodano.

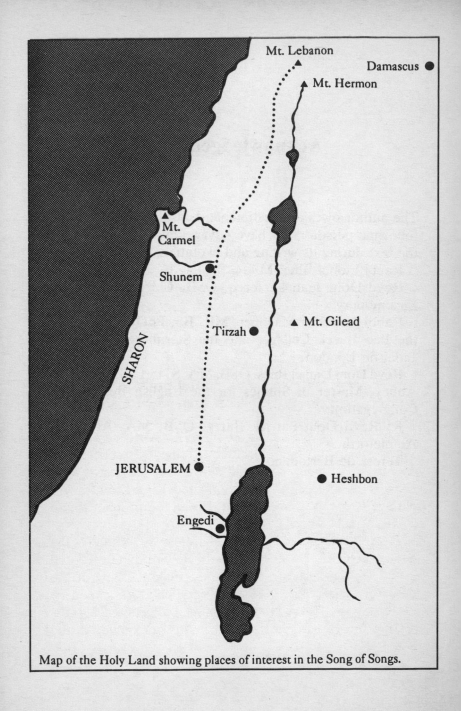

Map of the Holy Land showing places of interest in the Song of Songs.

Author's Note

The translation of the Song of Songs contained in *Love's Fugue* was made from the Hebrew by the author. Where the sense seemed to indicate the need for a different pointing, she has felt free to change the pointing of the Masoretic text which was agreed upon in the eighth–ninth century AD by leading Jewish scholars who determined the Hebrew letters and fixed the vowel signs – this is the Hebrew text found in most manuscripts.

Shulamitess
This is one of the titles given to the Bride in the Song, a name taken from the village from whence she came. Shulam can be identified with the ancient Shunem found in the Plain of Esdraelon, some miles north of Jezreel. This was part of the portion of the Tribe of Issachar; here too, the Philistines encamped before the final battle with King Saul; Abishag – who comforted King David in his old age – hailed from Shunem; Elisha the prophet found a lodging-place here.

The Hebrew word for Shulamitess is virtually the feminine form of Solomon. Both are intimately rooted in the Hebrew word for 'peace' – 'shalom'. Part of the thesis of this book is that it is a song of *peace* gained by exercising true love. King Solomon, the reputed author, betrays this peace and love, while it is personified in the Shulamitess.

A section of a relief from the royal palace at el-Amarna in Egypt (14th century BC), showing the women's house at the Pharaoh's court. The house is two storeyed.

Title and Prologue

1:1   The finest song of all, which is Solomon's.

BRIDE   *(of her true Beloved)*
1:2a   O, that he would kiss me
        with the kisses of his mouth!

BRIDE   *(recalling the words of her Beloved in former times)*
1:2b   'More delightful than wine is your love!
1:3a   Delightful, the fragrance of your perfume!'

BRIDE   *(responding to her absent Beloved and addressing him directly)*
1:3b   Your name is perfume poured out!
1:3c   That is why the maidens love you!
1:4a   Draw me after you!
        Let us make haste!
1:4b   The King has forced me
        into his rooms!

DAUGHTERS OF JERUSALEM *(addressing the Bride in admiration)*
1:4c   We will be glad
        and rejoice in you!
        We will recall your love
        more delightful than wine!
        Rightly do they love you!

Title and Prologue

'Love's Fugue' or 'The Finest Song of All' comes to us in the biblical book named after its opening verse: 'The Song of Songs, which is Solomon's.' King Solomon has been named by tradition as the author, but certain scholars prefer to give the period of the Second Temple in the fifth or fourth century before Christ as the date of its authorship.

It has been called the 'choicest' of all songs. Rabbinical interpretation as found in the Midrash (ancient Jewish commentary on part of the scriptures) teaches that on account of its extensive use of parallels, this song is a twofold song repeatedly singing Israel's praise of God and God's praise of Israel; and it is a twofold song in its beauty and holiness.

Laying aside all other approaches to this 'holy of holies' among biblical songs, I want to pursue a single line of thought concerning its content and message. This song is the Song of the Feminine. Among all the songs in the scriptures it voices uniquely the aspirations and desires of Woman. At least sixty-five of its 117 verses are the utterances of the feminine heart, telling her story, her plight, her yearnings, her strength and her frailty, her oppression and her flight to freedom. Above all it is the song of her unfolding fidelity in love.

In the Bible there is no other song of a woman which can be compared to the sheer artistry, integrity and length of this song. Even the Song of Deborah resounding with boldness, vigour and invincible faith, is not the song of Deborah alone, but of Deborah and Barak. Esther's

Prayer, arising pathetically like a lone cry in the night, cannot compare with this song for boldness and daring, as its melodies and cadences burst upon our ears revealing to us the naked heart of Everywoman and unveiling the intense intimacy of the love of this lone woman of the song.

The Songs of Hannah, Judith, and even Mary, are of a different order – being splendid shafts of soaring song lifting us into the circle of their closeness to their God. This song is more complex; its aim is completely other. It entices us into the inmost heart of every woman at her most vulnerable, yet most powerful, point, into the meaning and the mode of her love.

This is the finest song of all on account of the quality and quantity of the parallels it uses to proclaim and celebrate the essence of feminine love. As the rich abundance of these parallels unfolds with the lilting progress of the song, they toss into the mind a scintillating array of truths which yield ever new and challenging meanings the more we ponder and sing them over to ourselves.

Before listening to the text of the Prologue, I want to say a few words about the choice of the title – *Love's Fugue* – which I have given to this commentary on the Song. Frequent meditation on the Song has led me to coin this title. There is a phrase which occurs in the first of the five songs: 'I compare you, my love to . . .' Meditating on the Song leads naturally to the movement of comparing its content and progression to other forms of music – even to more modern, intricate forms. The fundamental 'movement' of the Bride in the Song – the 'movement' that characterises her from the opening of the Prologue to the concluding verses five songs later – is that of being 'in flight', either 'in flight to', or 'in flight from', someone or something. The complex interplay of 'in flight to' or 'in flight from' is the very fabric of which the work is composed, and gives to the Song its peculiar fascination.

Musically a 'flight' bears the name of a fugue: a composition developed from one or more short themes according to the rules and resources of counterpoint, with each of the parts being important to the whole. As Maria Luigi Cherubini, that master of counterpoint, tells us: 'All that a good composer ought to know may find its place in a fugue; it is the *type of every piece of music* . . . ' The essential elements of a fugue are: the subject, the answer, the counter-subject. These elements, after the first enunciation of the subject or main theme, progress in various ways through a series of 'entries' and expositions until the whole is brought to its conclusion in the final group. The 'flight' of the basic musical theme with its answers and counter-subject in various treatments through the entire fugue constitutes the main appeal and fascination in such music: there is always movement, the arising of a new variation or counterpoint weaving a kind of call to closer attention to the fundamental message, highlighting it more clearly.

As the fugue is the type of every piece of music, so this song, Love's Fugue, is the type of every woman's love experience. It is, in its own right, an authentic fugue, beginning with the principal theme; then comes the answer, the counter-subject and all the intricate variations of each as Love's Fugue progresses through its Prologue, each of the five songs, and comes to rest in the Epilogue.

The Song powerfully evokes other associations. In particular it can be described as *the type of the experience of love as it could be for Everywoman*. For in this song we encounter authentic feminine love sung and celebrated as an ideal in the midst of complete realism.

In the Prologue we are introduced briefly and poignantly to the subject of the Song's theme and to the answer, the counter-subject, as well as to an 'episode' which characterises certain fugues. There is another point about this Prologue. It is best understood not only as the Prologue to the entire work of five songs, but as being the Prologue to each of the five songs in turn. It is this understanding of the Prologue that will be used in this exposition of the Song.

So let us now begin to sing with the woman of the Song, the Bride, the song of her heart. As we sing it with her, our awareness of its meaning will grow – her vibrant reality will unfold like a living process.

> O, that he would kiss me
> with the kisses of his mouth! (1:2a)

These opening notes of the Song leading into the melody lilting with poignancy fall into the first cadences enfolding the fundamental note of every feminine heart: *the desire to be loved*. This is unashamedly the authentic voice of the feminine, singing out that quivering flame of desire which throbs so ardently in the heart of Everywoman that it can never be suppressed.

This is true of the feminine heart on whatever level we care to consider it – as a collective concept, as the Church, or as the individual soul in relation to its Creator, to Christ, or in its search for human love. This desire, itself a kind of spiritual flight, soaring aloft on the movement of the song, is the desire to be loved by her ideal counterpart – the ideal Beloved; yet not in any mode, or any counterpoint, but in the one specific mode which she defines as 'the kisses of his mouth'.

The image of receiving a kiss or kisses betokens a relationship brimming over with peace, and this is indicated in the scriptural dedication at the beginning of this song.[1] A relationship full of tenderness, reverence, docility, mutual surrender and non-violent openness in love. It implies mutual acceptance in freedom, fearless intimacy and an innate equality of being.

In the absence of the actual desired kisses of her Beloved, the Bride's desire is continually enkindled by recalling the memory of the words of love uttered by the same mouth by which she now yearns to be kissed:

More delightful than wine is your love!
Delightful, the fragrance of your perfume! (1:2b, 3a)

This intimate memory is the music of the fugue's 'answer' to the initial theme or subject. The subject is the feminine 'desire to be loved'. Her memory stirs itself and thus responds providing the 'real answer' – her ideal counterpart or Beloved is *he who loves her*. The twofold comparison of her love as delightful wine and her perfume as delightful fragrance, forms a figurative parallel which reaffirms that her desire to be loved is not in vain, for *her Beloved loves her*.

The first two themes of the fugue thus being introduced: the subject (the feminine desire to be loved) and the answer (the masculine need to love), the Bride proceeds to express her delight in being loved and in her Beloved with a superb response to her Beloved's compliment to her.

Your name is perfume poured out!
That is why the maidens love you! (1:3b,c)

His very name spreads its appealing perfume around, causing him to be loved by many maidens.

Desire kindles desire. So now the Bride is once more poised for another flight of desire, but this time her yearning has a double edge. There now enters into the fugue a tremulous tone of urgency in the face of danger. She calls to her Beloved:

Draw me after you!
Let us make haste!
The King has forced me
into his rooms! (1:4a,b)

The Bride's peril is revealed in these words. Her élan of
yearning to be loved by her ideal counterpart is not only
fed by her desire to be loved, but with equal intensity by
her desire to be delivered from danger – and instinctively
she knows that her Beloved is the only one who can
deliver her. The real situation is not one of untrammelled
freedom to respond to authentic love, but one where lust
has stolen by force her liberty and dignity.

Love becomes all the sweeter once lust has imposed
its greed for power, domination and pleasure. There is
no trial more crucifying for one who seeks and desires
love than to be coerced, compelled and ensnared by lust.
This is the fate of the Bride in the Song. Instead of the
freedom to be loved by her ideal counterpart, she has
fallen a victim to the lust of another who was a treacherous
usurper of virtue.

It is the extreme intensity of the Bride's appeal to
her Beloved to draw her after him and to make haste
that emphasises the radical peril arising from the King's
coercion, forcing her into his rooms. So now Love's Fugue
takes its keenly dramatic turn with this introduction of the
third element in its development – the counter-subject.

From this point on, the unfolding themes entering
and re-entering the fugue will focus on the flight of
the Bride to or with her true Beloved, or her flight
from the King who is the man of lust. Thus, love
and lust will appear and reappear in the counterpoint
of the song, with innumerable variations, depending
upon which theme is uppermost in the song – love
or lust. There could be no more strongly contrasted
or dramatic themes than love and lust to unveil to

its full depth the song of the feminine desire to be loved.

But no fugue is complete without its 'episodes' or 'interludes' which act as a musical catalyst to help refocus on the main themes. 'Love's Fugue' is no exception, and so we now meet what might be called the 'bystanders' view' of the proceedings in the chorus now sung by those enigmatic personalities, the 'Daughters of Jerusalem':

> We will be glad
> and rejoice in you!
> We will recall your love
> more delightful than wine!
> Rightly do they love you! (1:4c)

Three points are made in the chorus. These outsiders are witnessing something that is for them a cause of gladness and rejoicing. They are deeply interested in the kind of love shown by the Bride and want to recall it – in every sense of the word, having heard that it is more delightful than wine. Finally they reveal their own ambiguity by using the word 'love' in conjunction with both the true Beloved and the King: for we have already heard how contrary are the relationships of these two men to the Bride. The term 'love' can hardly be applied to both in the same way: the Beloved's love is authentic; the King's 'love' is spurious.

Thus, in four brief verses the Prologue sets out the basic pattern of the Song:

(a) the subject (the feminine desire to be loved);
(b) the answer (the masculine need to love);
(c) the counter-subject (the power of lust);
(d) the episode (the outside reflection on the themes).

We must now begin to listen to the unfolding fugue in the First Song of the Bride.

Notes

Prologue

1 Song, v.1: The Song of Songs which is Solomon's. The name Solomon means peace, although the King fails to live up to this designation in the Bride's regard.

The First Song of the Bride

BRIDE   *(to the Daughters of Jerusalem)*
1:5   I am black, but I am beautiful,
            O ye Daughters of Jerusalem,
            like the tents of Kedar!
            like the curtains of Solomon!

1:6   Do not gaze at me
            because I am black,
            for the sun has burnt me;

            for my mother's sons
            burnt with anger against me,
            they put me to guard the vineyards;
            but my own vineyard
            I failed to guard!

BRIDE   *(to her absent Beloved)*
1:7   Tell me, O you whom my soul so loves,
            where do you pasture your flock?
            Where do you rest it at noon?
            For why should I be as one veiled
            by the flocks of your friends?

DAUGHTERS OF JERUSALEM *(speaking sarcastically*
            to the Bride)
1:8   If you do not know
            O fairest of women!
            Go, follow in the tracks of the flock
            and near to the tents of the shepherds
            there pasture your flock!

KING SOLOMON *(to the Bride)*

1:9   O my love, you I compare
to a prancing mare
in the chariot of Pharaoh!

1:10   How beautiful your cheeks
with circlets of beads!
your neck with its strings of beads!

1:11   We will make you circlets of gold
all studded with silver!

BRIDE   *(Of the King, but musing on her Beloved)*

1:12   While the King was on his couch
my spikenard exhaled its fragrance.

1:13   My Beloved is to me
a bundle of myrrh
lodging in my bosom.

1:14   A cluster of henna
in the vineyards of Engeddi,
so is my Beloved to me!

KING SOLOMON *(to the Bride)*

1:15   Behold, my love,
your eyes are doves!
How fair you are,
Behold, so very fair!

BRIDE   *(to her absent Beloved, and against the King)*

1:16   Behold, my Beloved,
it is you who are fair!
It is you who indeed are delightful!
Also, our couch is of leaves,

1:17   the beams of our houses are cedars,
and our ceilings are cypresses!

BRIDE   *(yearning for her rustic country life)*

2:1   I am a flower of the field,

a lily of the valleys!

KING SOLOMON *(recalling her and flattering her)*
2:2   In the midst of the maidens is my love,
           like a lily in the midst of thorns!

BRIDE   *(ignoring the King and continuing to muse on
           her Beloved)*
2.3   Like an apple tree
           among the trees of the wood,
           so is my Beloved
           among the youths.
           Beneath his shade
           I delighted to stay,
           and his fruit was sweet
           to my taste.
2:4   He brought me to his festal house
           and over me
           his banner unfurled is love.

2:5   Strengthen me with cakes!
           Refresh me with apples!
           For I am wounded with love!

2:6   O that his left hand
           were under my head,
           and his right hand embracing me!

BRIDE   *(chorus)*
2:7   I adjure you, O Daughters of Jerusalem!
           By the hinds and gazelles of the field,
           that you do not arouse nor awaken love
           until it pleases to awake!

The First Song of the Bride (1:5–2:7)

The First Song of the Bride continues Love's Fugue unfolding the subject of authentic love and the counter-subject of lust. There is a natural division in this song: the first part (1:5–8) sings of the Bride's nascent love and desire amid sibling jealousy, while the second part expounds the first trials of this love as it encounters the advances of lust. Each part ends with its own chorus.

The First Part: love's initial trials and sibling jealousy

The First Song continues from the point reached in the Prologue. We remember that the Bride was proclaiming her state of captivity and oppression. We remember too the bystanders in the persons of the Daughters of Jerusalem making ambiguous statements about her. Now the Bride responds to these Daughters of Jerusalem and takes up her song in a special way, singing of the development of her feminine love and desire. It is fitting that she does this at this precise moment in the first of her five songs.

The two opening verses of this First Song begin with the Bride singing to us her story, of who she is and of her experiences in recent times:

> I am black, but I am beautiful,
> O ye Daughters of Jerusalem,

like the tents of Kedar!
like the curtains of Solomon!

Do not gaze at me
because I am black,
for the sun has burnt me;

for my mother's sons
burnt with anger against me,
they put me to guard the vineyards;
but my own vineyard
I failed to guard! (1:5–6)

Here we listen to a sequence of thought bearing a self-revelation which is extremely important; in fact crucial to the understanding of the Bride at this stage and also later on in the other songs.

First of all she describes herself:

I am black, but I am beautiful,
O ye Daughters of Jerusalem,
Black, like the tents of Kedar!
Beautiful, like the curtains of Solomon!

The Bride then proceeds to describe *why* she is so black, because for that race and that nationality to be black in this sense of the word was not to be beautiful.

The word 'black' which she uses to identify, designate and describe herself, is pregnant with meaning which enables us to grasp the whole sequence of progression in the five songs. Elsewhere in the scriptures we encounter this same word, and notably in Psalm 110, verse 3, where we are told of this mysterious person of whom God declares: 'I have begotten you from *before the dawn.*' Thus the blackness of the Bride can be linked to that blackness characterising the darkest hour of the night just before dawn breaks.

This is precisely the significance of the word in this present context of the song. For the story of the Bride, as she tells it in these songs, is that of a young woman about to break forth from the darkness of ignorance about herself from her childhood state of lacking adult self-knowledge to the full day of deeper consciousness of who she is and the significance of the maturing of her womanhood. Thus, by using this key word 'black', as a kind of prelude, the Bride gives us a little glimpse of what is going to happen in the course of the five songs: the unfolding story of a young girl emerging from childhood and developing into womanhood. She also shows that she is neither unaware of nor divorced from reality in giving us this picture of herself.

She has taken up the challenge thrown down by the Daughters of Jerusalem in their chorus at the end of the Prologue. She tells them quite clearly that even though she is black, she is beautiful. In this statement of hers there is something of awakening self-awareness that is true, clear and convincing. Her blackness, she says, is like the tents of Kedar, which were traditionally made of black goat-skin. But her beauty, as she declares, is like the curtains of Solomon. Presumably she had never set eyes on the curtains of Solomon before. Now that she is his prisoner in his dwelling, she has ample opportunity to observe the shimmering luxury and beauty of his curtains, and is bold enough to compare her own beauty to such sumptuous furnishings of the King.

Then she goes on to describe how she became black:

> Do not gaze at me
> because I am black,
> for the sun has burnt me . . . (1:6a)

In other words, she is sunburnt because her mother's sons, her own brothers

> burnt with anger against me,
> they put me to guard the vineyards;
> but my own vineyard
> I failed to guard! (1:6b)

So as she sings, we discover that her story so far is not exactly one of a happy, carefree, country childhood. It is the story of discrimination against her by her own brothers. Just as the sun has scorched and burnt her with its unrelenting heat, so also has she been blackened and seared spiritually and emotionally by the male siblings of her family, as they burnt hot with anger and jealousy against her. They put her to guard their vineyards, and there, out on the hot hillside among the vines under the burning rays of the sun, she became badly sunburnt.

So her song tells us that she has already experienced in her own person and within her own family, a kind of oppression. Her present state of confinement and oppression is but another step in the journey of her life-experience. At the same time she is awakening to the harsh realities of life and lets us know that she too had failed by letting her own vineyard – a description of her own person, her own self – remain unguarded, unattended. She returns to this theme later, but for the moment she expresses a real regret that in her preoccupation with the oppression imposed on her by her brothers in having to guard their vineyards, she herself has been taken off-guard and has been captured by King Solomon's minions.

Why were her brothers so angry with her? Why did they try to curb her activity and control her behaviour? Why did they put her in a safe place, as it were, to guard their walled-in vineyards? According to verse 7 and its context I do not think we can say that they just did it because they imposed on their 'little sister', as they called her later on in the song. Rather they acted out of the kind of unspoken sibling rivalry and jealousy innate in older brothers, when they begin to see that their little sister is already receiving the attentions of a young shepherd in whom she is taking too much interest. They feel angry and jealous that she will perhaps escape soon from the close family circle, grow up and launch out into her own life and her own chosen and preferred relationships. So, as some older brothers are wont to do in such circumstances, they try to confine her on the family property and keep her well occupied.

Even so, they can never curb, control or oppress that awakening desire for true love in her, a desire she has already thrilled to in her association with that young shepherd who has so swiftly become her Beloved. As in the vineyards in her first state of oppression, so now in the tents and confines of King Solomon's quarters, her desire and her yearning fly out to that one, true Beloved of her soul:

> Tell me, O you whom my soul so loves,
> where do you pasture your flock?
> Where do you rest it at noon?
> For why should I be as one veiled
> by the flocks of your friends? (1:7)

In such ardent words she reveals the identity of her true Beloved. He is a country shepherd whom she probably met while she was still free to roam the hills of her home village; before her brothers' anger was aroused and they confined her to guarding the vineyards. The Bride here asks the question closest to her heart. Why must she act towards the one whom her soul loves as if she is an anonymous, obscure and veiled woman? Why does this nascent relationship have to be a secret? 'Why should I be as one veiled, by the flocks of your friends' instead of being able to be frank and open about this new relationship which she is discovering?

In such words the Bride reveals something of her story, with conviction and a certain youthful naivety, to the only audience she has in her present state of oppression and captivity – to the Daughters of Jerusalem. These haughty, sophisticated ladies-in-waiting to King Solomon's harem are perhaps nonplussed by this naive country girl's lack of response to the mode of life in the harem, and reply to her with sarcasm and some exasperation:

> If you do not know
> O fairest of women!
> Go, follow in the tracks of the flock
> and near to the tents of the shepherds
> there pasture your flock (1:8)

Their sarcasm is clearly revealed in their choice of words to describe the Bride after she has described herself – as 'I am black, but I am beautiful. I am black, for the sun has burnt me; I am black for my mother's sons burnt with anger against me.' To this self-description the Daughters of Jerusalem reply with biting sarcasm: 'O fairest of women . . . '

The word they used for 'fairest' is not the one used by the Bride for 'beautiful'. There is dark beauty and there is fair beauty. When we proclaim someone fair in this sense, we mean that they are not dark. So there is sarcasm in the words flung at the Bride. There is also exasperation, because these worldly women would really be rather glad to be rid of this country girl; her kind of character and her kind of beauty do not fit happily into their milieu and its activities. Perhaps they are beginning to wish King Solomon had not abducted her, for she does not look like going along with his desires.

There is a good deal in human life and in the maturing feminine experience that is the counterpart of the song so far. This holds true for the Church, as well as for the individual soul beginning to be awakened to respond to the mysterious inner call of love uttered by the true Shepherd.

Whether we consider the feminine in general, the Church, or more specifically the individual soul, life has never been completely smooth and unruffled. Dawn is ever about to break. The memory holds within itself those images and experiences of oppression, injustice and difficulty coming from the members of the 'family circle'. There has often been the need for the deepest secrets of the heart to be veiled and hidden from those most immediately around us.

There is also the experience of a certain sarcasm, scepticism and exasperation from the worldly-wise and supercilious when faced with the awakening desire of authentic feminine love: with the bridal mystery of the Church throughout history as well as with the inexplicable awakening consciousness of the value of the relationship with the ideal beloved in the heart of every woman unfolding into maturity.

The worldly-wise cannot grasp the deep meaning of life, of desire, of purity of love, of the need to be faithful in love, which stirs and quickens in the heart of every woman. This impasse arises because the true Beloved does not make himself present, visibly and tangibly. The worldly-wise therefore act unjustly, discriminate against and oppress the Bride as she struggles for maturity in love.

But for the Bride, the Beloved is 'seen' as absent. There has been an experience, however dimly perceived, of being loved by him, that can never be forgotten. It is this experience which the Bride in this song recounts as her nascent, free relationship with the shepherd who leads, protects and nurtures his flock at noon – the zenith of the day's wakefulness. For the Bride, her maturing life-experience is already envisioned as something reaching

out from the black 'darkness before dawn to the full pleni-
tude of light and rest at noon'. This flight from darkness
before dawn to the brightness of noontide light and rest
is part of the inherent movement of Love's Fugue. In this
first half of the First Song of the Bride we hear already
the progressions and cadences of authentic love conveyed
through the movement from pre-dawn darkness, shadow
and anticipation towards the full flux of light at high noon;
in the desire for full maturity of authentic love given and
received in freedom, mutuality and unveiled presence.

As we progress through the Five Songs of the Bride we
become fascinated at the interplay of images of night and
darkness yielding gradually to images of light and freedom
in love.

In this part of the First Song, there is another image
so precious in the religious history of the Bible – the
image of the *vineyard*. How often Israel was called the
vineyard of the Lord – his chosen vineyard! We also know
the sorry story of Israel as the vineyard of the Lord. Psalm
77 relates how the Lord carried his vineyard out of Egypt
to plant it anew in the Promised Land. In other words,
how he rescued it from slavery and oppression and found
it a new home where he replanted and tended it with
loving care. But then, the brothers came and ruined it.
However, finally the Beloved, the True Beloved, did
come, proclaiming himself the very Vine and ourselves
the Branches. Thus the concept and the development
of the vineyard theme is of great importance both in
the song of the Bride and in the unfolding of salvation
history.

In a similar way the shepherd image is vital to Love's
Fugue and to salvation history. But for the worldly-wise,
sophisticated associates of the Daughters of Jerusalem,
the shepherd and his flock seem to stand only for
a simple, naive country way of life – one closed to
progress, culture, civilisation, in fact everything that

belongs to the superior way of life of King Solomon and his world.

So we have in these first few verses of the Bride's song a clear presentation of her story. There is something of the oppression she has already endured; there is something of the promise of what her maturing in love and desire will bring her. We learn from the outset that her true Beloved is loved in his absence, rather than the oppressor who has forced her into his own seductive presence.

We learn too of the kinds of trials which have to be endured on this feminine journey, at whatever level it is undertaken. There will be oppression and contradiction from within the family, from the siblings – especially the male siblings. There will be scorn and sarcasm from the jaded, embittered feminine in others who have become worldly-wise, and who resent and can no longer comprehend the sincere journey of the spirit. There will be the awareness that once this spiritually maturing awakening to love has begun, then many oppressions, bondages and abductions have to be surmounted and spurned, which can only be done successfully by fidelity to the vision and reality of the true Beloved.

The Second Part: the seductive advances of lust

This second part of the First Song of the Bride (1:9–2:7) brings us back abruptly to the Bride's present predicament. As the Bride continues her song we hear the processes of lust seeking to dominate and possess the Bride. This is followed by a poetic piece of sheer inspiration in which the Bride celebrates the delights of her Beloved before the final chorus in which she confronts the Daughters of Jerusalem for their worldly-wise stance.

It is the counter-subject of lust which dominates in the first movement of this part of the song which is extremely important and brings us right into the heart of the conflict between lust and love. Here the Bride shares with us her experience of lust's advances and the distinction between lust and love.

It seems necessary to give a brief resumé of the kind of movement the Bride experiences and works through in her first encounter with the King. There are three progressive stages and a final chorus combining to make a pattern showing how lust operates.

In contrast to the first half of this song where the Bride took the initiative and sang of her own story, it is the King who takes the initiatives and makes the advances in this second half. He does this in three steps, and to each one the Bride reacts strongly. This entire movement is an exposition of the qualities and techniques of lust in contrast to the description, reactions and aspirations of love. As we move through this part of the song the dominant voice in the beginning is that of lust. But gradually that voice stammers into silence, and the voice of the Bride proclaiming true love rises to a crescendo. The climax comes in the final chorus with her challenge to these ambiguous creatures, the Daughters of Jerusalem, when she flatly accuses them of conniving with the King and tells them that they ought not to try to tamper with the authentic movements of love.

These verses bring us into the arena of a conflict and encounter between lust and love. We now need to look closely at this in order to delineate the stages and the techniques of lust in the song. In so doing we need to remember that according to the Bride's own story she is a young girl emerging into maturity. She stands for the feminine experience of life. At this stage of development a crucially important distinction enters the feminine experience – on a physical and emotional level as well as on the spiritual. We all know it in some way or other. The desire to be loved awakens within the heart, and then an encounter with lust comes from without, from another. The story of life from the feminine point of view depends on how each one handles this encounter, and on the continuing choices consequent upon this initial stance. In this song the Bride clearly makes a radical choice for authentic love. But she has to confront the temptations of lust as follows:

The assessment

The King moves on stage as the prince of power, worldly poise and the figure of seductive darkness. He begins by making an assessment of the Bride's personality, her character and her qualities:

> O my love, you I compare
> to a prancing mare
> in the chariot of Pharaoh! (1:9)

Most commentators on this verse inform us in rather lyrical tones that in those days there was no more beautiful beast than the Egyptian horse with its flowing mane, fiery vigour and power, and swift fineness of speed. So the King is telling the Bride of her beauty, that he is discerning that she is a high-spirited creature, the best going, in fact. But concealed in this statement is the subtlety of domination and oppression – and even a hint of cruelty. The Bride is a mare in the chariot of Pharaoh; that is to say, she is broken in, she is harnessed between two shafts and the reins of power are held by a person of power – she cannot escape. In other words, she is reduced to a thing, an object, a possession.

To this approach the Bride makes no response whatever, so the seducer, sure of himself, advances on the
three stages of lust's temptations.

Stage One (1:10,11)

> How beautiful your cheeks
> with circlets of beads!
> your neck with its strings of beads!
> We will make you circlets of gold
> all studded with silver!

We all know the old, familiar story: 'You are very nice,
but your simple adornments are not a patch on what I
will give you. After all, I am wealthy – and so you can
have gold and silver in exchange for your simple beads
purchased at some country market.' It is the old, facile
temptation of the promise of riches and wealth to seduce
innocence and simplicity.

Circlets of gold, studded with silver, when they are
offered the Bride close on the heels of the image of
her as a prancing mare in the chariot of Pharaoh, sound
very much as if the bands of gold and studs of silver with
which he would harness the Bride are to be more rigid
and rigorous than those of the mare. Many of us have
seen horses' harnesses on parade with rings of gold and
studs of silver; and they are pretty heavy, weighing the
poor beasts down. In other words, the flattery in verse
10 leads to greater enslavement in verse 11 under the
guise of the false promise of wealth and adornment –
if, of course, the victim of seduction accepts the promise
and the flattery.

There is still silence on the part of the Bride.

Stage Two (1:12–14)

The seducer's words yield to his actions and the Bride's
reactions in the next three verses:

> While the King was on his couch
> my spikenard exhaled its fragrance.

> My Beloved is to me
> a bundle of myrrh
> lodging in my bosom.
> A cluster of henna
> in the vineyards of Engeddi,
> so is my Beloved to me!

The King now resorts to actions, not words. He has forced the Bride into his inner room where she is alone with him, and he is on his couch. The Bride, however, takes the initiative now. Everything within her has been alerted. This is not where she belongs, so she puts the King in his place by saying:

> While the King was on *his* couch
> my spikenard exhaled its fragrance.

That is to say, 'There's seduction here, but there is also distance', and the fragrance of the Bride is something different from lust and its enticements. She continues to explain and proclaim that lust holds no appeal for her because she already has her own experience of true love in the person of her Beloved. She expresses this in the beautiful image of the inward intimacy and power of memory on which love is nurtured giving it the strength to resist even the powerfully seductive advances of lust:

> My Beloved is to me
> a bundle of myrrh
> lodging in my bosom.
> A cluster of henna
> in the vineyards of Engeddi,
> so is my Beloved to me!

Stage Three (1:15)

This is the return to flattery on the part of the seducer:

> Behold, my love,
> your eyes are doves!
> How fair you are,
> Behold, so very fair!

The seducer knows from long experience that a woman's weakest point is her openness to flattery. However the Bride in this instance does not yield to it. She reacts rather by praising the delightfulness and fairness of her Beloved in dramatic terms. By making and continuing the clear distinction she had begun in verse 12, 'while the King was on *his* couch', she moves on to sing, concerning herself and her Beloved, of '*our* couch, *our* houses and *our* ceilings', she identifies herself with her former rustic, sylvan lifestyle with her Beloved.

   Thus she emphatically states that she wants nothing to do with the wealth, the sophistication and the kind of behaviour that belong to luxuriously curtained rooms and a king's couch. She ends with a simple statement of self-identity which really says 'I do not belong here, I belong elsewhere in simplicity and purity of heart.'

> I am a flower of the field,
> a lily of the valleys! (2:1)

Thus the song moves us forward to the point where the King seducer is himself forced to reassess the Bride. Somehow he seems to have failed in his original assessment and in the successive temptations. He even attempts to coin part of her own imagery in this reassessment of her person:

> In the midst of the maidens is my love,
> like a lily in the midst of thorns! (2:2)

This is perhaps the most ambiguous and difficult statement in the whole of this song. In order to understand it, let us take the second line first.

'A lily in the midst of thorns' is obviously taken from 'a lily of the valley' which the Bride used of herself. What does it mean to be a lily in the midst of thorns? We can look at it in several ways.

A lily surrounded by thorns is a lily imprisoned. It cannot move or escape without tearing its delicate petals to pieces, and having its fragile beauty destroyed by the cruelty of the thorns. Perhaps this is one of the meanings that the King is putting into his words – he is uttering a kind of threat to this helpless, fragile victim of his lust: 'You are trapped, you can't escape; the maidens, or Daughters of Jerusalem, who are my minions have charge of you, encircle you tightly – so do not try to escape!'

There is another way of assessing this statement. The thorns around the lily mean that he, the seducer, cannot get at the lily either, or he too will be pricked and torn by the encircling thorns. This interpretation lends an intriguing colour to the parallel which the first line makes to balance the second:

> In the midst of the maidens is my love,
> like a lily in the midst of thorns!

This confirms that the maidens must be the Daughters of Jerusalem, his own servants, and thus the comparison is unflattering both to them and to himself. His own maidens are preventing him from approaching this fragile lily whom he thought was entirely in his power. By this comparison the Daughters of Jerusalem are seen again to be unsatisfactory characters, awkward bystanders on life's scene. On whose side are they? Are they on the side of the King, their master? Or are they on the side of the Bride, his prisoner? The King himself is unsure.

The Bride at this point takes up the song once more and in a new flight of love's desire sings her eulogy of her Beloved using images taken from her former rustic life. She sings of freedom, festivity, mutuality and harmony. She sings too of that undying wound of love with which she feels so deeply afflicted – the more so now that her desired union with her Beloved seems irreversibly beyond her reach. She becomes more daring than heretofore and sings boldly of the longed-for embrace of her Beloved:

> Like an apple tree
> among the trees of the wood,
> so is my Beloved
> among the youths.
> Beneath his shade
> I delighted to stay,
> and his fruit was sweet
> to my taste.
> He brought me to his festal house
> and over me
> his banner unfurled is love.
>
> Strengthen me with cakes!
> Refresh me with apples!
> For I am wounded with love!
>
> O that his left hand
> were under my head,
> and his right hand embracing me! (2:3–6)

This flight of love's desire sung and over, the Bride, like the King, turns her attention once more to those perplexing personalities on the sidelines of the scene, the Daughters of Jerusalem. She is beginning to see through them and their activities, and she does not like what she sees. She confronts them, challenges them, adjuring them not to tamper with the innate, intimate movements and workings of love:

> I adjure you, O Daughters of Jerusalem!
> By the hinds and gazelles of the field,
> that you do not arouse nor awaken love
> until it pleases to awake! (2:7)

Boldly, and with daring, this simple country maid takes it upon herself to upbraid these sophisticated, worldly women. In their world lust and coercion cohabit. But lust is not love. Love belongs to a different sphere of reality, life and activity altogether. Love is as free as the hinds and gazelles of the field – it is no Egyptian mare harnessed tightly to Pharaoh's chariot!

With this splendid chorus upholding the freedom of love this First Song of the Bride ends. We have heard its progression from the initial, intimate self-revelation of the Bride as she recounts her own story, to her first encounter with the coercive power of the seducer, the prince or king of darkness and his lust. She has sung of her own attitude of resistance to his temptations as well as her further flights of desire for her true Beloved. Finally we have heard her coolly daring to spurn and adjure those bystanders in life whose task seemed to be to cajole her to yield to lust rather than remain steadfast to love.

The Bride now stands out before us quite clearly and distinctly as a young woman of refinement, who is opting for truth and fidelity in love, though the odds are against her. She is in captivity and not free to move out of the closed circle of lustful pressure and oppression, but she makes it abundantly clear that her options are along the lines of fidelity to her first Beloved.

The Second Song of the Bride

BRIDE   *(In her dream she hears, sees and cries out to her Beloved, and in return he sings to her and calls her to escape from her royal captor)*

2:8   Hark! my Beloved!
Behold! He is coming!
Leaping on the mountains!
Bounding o'er the hills!

2:9   Like a gazelle, my Beloved,
or like a young hart!
Behold, he is here!
Looking through the windows,
peering through the lattices,
standing at our wall!

2:10   My Beloved sang,
and he called to me:

BELOVED *(singing to his Bride)*
Arise, my love, my fair one,
arise and come away!

2:11   For, lo, the winter is past,
the rain is over and gone!

2:12   The flowers appear in the land,
the time of pruning has come;
and the voice of the turtle-dove
is heard in our land!

2:13   The fig-tree ripens her unripe figs,
and the vine's tender grapes

exhale their fragrance!
Arise my love! Come, my fair one,
and come away!

2:14   O my dove!
in the clefts of the rock,
in the covert of the cliff,
show me your face!
Let me hear your voice!
for sweet is your voice,
and beautiful your face!

BRIDE   *(answering her Beloved, letting him know she
is trapped and imprisoned by deceivers)*
2:15   Catch the foxes for us!
The young foxes that ravage the vineyards,
for our vineyards have tender grapes.

2:16   My Beloved is mine,
and I am his:
among the lilies
he takes his delight!
2:17   Ere the dawn breeze stirs,
and the shadows take flight,
turn, my Beloved!
Be like a gazelle,
or like a young hart,
upon the mountains of Bether!

3:1   By night, upon my bed,
I sought him whom my soul so loves;
I sought him but I found him not.

3:2   So, now I will arise,
I will go about the city;
in the streets and in the squares,
I will seek him whom my soul so loves;
I sought him but I found him not!

3:3   The watchmen who go about the city
found me. (I said to them:)
Have you seen him
whom my soul so loves?

3:4   I had scarcely passed them by
when I found him whom my soul so loves;
I caught hold of him,
and would not let him go,
until I brought him
to my mother's house,
even to the inner room
of her who conceived me.

BRIDE   *chorus*
3:5   I adjure you, O Daughters of Jerusalem!
By the hinds and gazelles of the field,
that you do not arouse nor awaken love
until it pleases to awake!

The Second Song of the Bride (2:8–3:5)

Prologue

Bride:

> O, that he would kiss me
> with the kisses of his mouth!
>
> 'More delightful than wine is your love!
> Delightful, the fragrance of your perfume!'
>
> Your name is perfume poured out!
> That is why the maidens love you!
> Draw me after you!
> Let us make haste!
> The King has forced me
> into his rooms!

The Prologue to Love's Fugue finds its fitting place once more as it is repeated at the beginning of the Second Song of the Bride. Her First Song describes in unforgettable melodies her first encounter with the lust of the seducer King who has forced her into his rooms. No wonder her desire goes out even more ardently to her true Beloved, yearning for his presence and support.

*   *   *

The Second Song of the Bride is in marked contrast to the First where the counter-subject in the fugue is dominant for most of the song. In the Second Song Love's Fugue takes up again the subject of feminine love and its true answer – the love of the Beloved for the Bride. So the whole mood changes dramatically and as we listen we are drawn into another world altogether.

It is night again. The Bride is back in her own quarters in the King's harem. After the trauma of the day she now falls fitfully into sleep and also into the time-hallowed remedy of all lovers deprived of the loved person – she seeks solace in her anguish of soul by dreaming of her Beloved. This dream is the love-dream *par excellence*.

This song can be seen as 'the perfect love-dream', representing that inward activity of the Bride in her state of crisis. We all know that intensity of desire in our waking life, as well as deprivation of a desired person or object, can lead us in our dreams to reclaim and re-enter into possession of that desired person or object. For the Bride there is a respite in the advances of the seductive King and in her fitful sleep the inner world of fantasy and dream springs unhindered into action.

Her dream is centred, naturally, on her Beloved, and so the language of love begins to emerge very powerfully in this Second Song. The dream, as she sings it, falls into three main sections, and the whole concludes with the now expected chorus of the Bride.

Introduction: the Bride's desire for the Beloved (2:8–10)

The Bride's dream opens with her intense desire for her Beloved portrayed in lively imagery of his coming to her, and even being already with her. The activity and pattern of desire in arousing inward fantasy and dream images that are so vivid as to be more real than reality, is an authentic phenomenon. We can see it here in the Bride dreaming of her Beloved. It was also true of the bride Israel, in bondage and captivity, dreaming of her husband, Yahweh. It holds true of the bride Church, who, especially in times of persecution, dreams more vividly of the glory and majesty of her Bridegroom, than in times of ease and prosperity. The more that outward adversity presses upon the individual soul, seeking to be wedded to Christ, the more she will tend to recreate inwardly, through love's desire, those rich images of her relationship with her true Beloved, and in them find a wellspring of strength to persevere on her journey.

The Bride's dream takes place at night. Here night is the image of oppression, obscurity, darkness and captivity. And so, in the dream the opposites to darkness, obscurity and captivity, present themselves vibrantly:

> Hark! my Beloved!
> Behold! He is coming!
> Leaping on the mountains!
> Bounding o'er the hills!
>
> Like a gazelle, my Beloved,
> or like a young hart!
> Behold, he is here!
> Looking through the windows,
> peering through the lattices,
> standing at our wall! (2:8–9)

These are images of great freedom and agility. The mountains and hills can be seen as the great obstacles to love, the oppressions and captivities preventing love – the very situation at present weighing down the Bride so hopelessly. But her Beloved leaps over them all effortlessly, like a gazelle or a young hart, both creatures famous for their energy and agility. In such stirring words the Bride sings joyfully and thrillingly that her Beloved is coming in search for her, even as her desires leap up and out to him over the impossible obstacles that have been placed between them by the King seducer.

The essential flight of desire for her Beloved arising from the heart of the Bride finds in this dream its authentic counterpart and answer in the way she depicts the Beloved in full flight towards her, searching for her in the night. Her dream ardour sees and hears him as truly present to her:

> Behold, he is here!
> Looking through the windows,
> peering through the lattices,
> standing at our wall!

He is searching for her in the night and yet hidden within the text are images of light which his presence brings. The 'peering through the lattices' means literally glistening or sparkling – glistering through the crevices, through the chinks in the window curtains. So the Beloved, in his coming to her, brings light, the light of life, love and hope.

Her Beloved in the dream does not simply come and look – he does something else, something which convinces her even more surely that it is really her true Beloved who has thus searched out and discovered her whereabouts. He sings to her. He sings in the way that all lovers have sung to each other since the beginning of time. He serenades her with a song that only he could sing of events and scenes that touch upon and recall her present situation as well as former times together with him.

The Beloved's serenade: the former vineyard scene revisited (2:10–14)

> My Beloved sang,
> and he called to me:
>
> Arise, my love, my fair one,
> arise and come away! (2:10)

Relief floods into her soul. These are the words, this is the invitation she has been longing to hear, yearning to hear it from his lips. To be set free from the encircling chains of captivity and be able to arise freely, and flee away with him – this is all her desire. His words tell her that he too knows it is her desire. Her heart thrills at his song.

Her Beloved continues his serenade, reconstructing another scene, another image of darkness yielding to light and life – a symbol of his own presence with her now – he sings of winter awakening into springtime:

> . . . lo, the winter is past,
> the rain is over and gone!
> The flowers appear in the land,
> the time of pruning has come;
> and the voice of the turtle-dove
> is heard in our land!
>
> The fig-tree ripens her unripe figs,
> and the vine's tender grapes
> exhale their fragrance!
> Arise my love! Come, my fair one,
> and come away!

The Beloved's serenade recreates for her that original vineyard and garden scene where they had first met. It is spring, the time of hope, the time of love, the time of the resurgence of life. In singing of the pristine beauty of spring the Beloved is recalling those first thrilling encounters in the vineyard when the Bride's love for him was first awakened like a spring flower or a tender grape setting on the vine when the blossom begins to fall. This vineyard image is so important to the understanding of the song, for it frequently recurs as a symbol of the Bride herself. Her Beloved's serenade continues:

> O my dove!
> in the clefts of the rock,
> in the covert of the cliff,
> show me your face!
> Let me hear your voice!
> for sweet is your voice,
> and beautiful your face! (2:14)

There is a quality of ardour and sincerity about this part of the Beloved's serenade. He is genuinely searching for his Love. He is recapturing in song his earlier search when she had been put into her brothers' vineyard, and he had persistently sought her, trying to get a glimpse of her through the clefts and coverts of the cliff-like rocky wall surrounding the vineyard. As she hears his voice now, and his song, she thrills at the reviving memory of his words to her in those former days – he so longs to hear her voice and see her face.

It is an ideal dream, but like all dreams it cannot last for ever. Even as she continues dreaming, the rich contentment fades and other images flow in and out of her dream. First of all comes a dramatic image arising from her deep awareness of her present state of oppression and captivity.

The shifting fantasies of the Bride's dream (2:15–3:4)

> Catch the foxes for us!
> The young foxes that ravage the vineyards,
> for our vineyards have tender grapes. (2:15)

The Bride cries out, starting up in her dream. Her cry is not specifically directed to her Beloved; it is rather a cry in general, the cry of one unwillingly in bondage and under oppression. 'Catch the oppressors, catch the wily foxes and deliver me from them. Deliver me from the young foxes that ravage and tear apart my person, my freedom, my awakening love for my Beloved!'

In her repeated cry to be delivered from the evil foxes we see that even in her dream world the Bride makes a distinction between the big foxes and the little foxes that cause her oppression. In this song the chief foxes causing her great oppression, danger and peril in her life are certainly King Solomon and his minions. But even in her dream she is not forgetful of the 'little foxes' within her own family: her brothers who had tried to harm her by putting her to guard their vineyards which had led to her neglecting her own.

Dreams speak the truth. They cannot lie. In her dream the Bride cries out for deliverance from these ravaging foxes because basically their rapacious activities are aimed at destroying the purity and freedom of the mutual love between herself and her Beloved:

> Catch the foxes for us! . . . For
> my Beloved is mine,
> and I am his:
> among the lilies
> he takes his delight! (2:15–16)

The next fantasm that flits into her dream and then flows swiftly out of it again is one which highlights another aspect of love's flight of desire:

> Ere the dawn breeze stirs,
> and the shadows take flight,
> turn, my Beloved!
> Be like a gazelle,
> or like a young hart,
> upon the mountains of Bether! (2:17)

This verse shows us that even in her dream consciousness the Bride is somehow obscurely aware that this present dream meeting with her Beloved must come to an end before daybreak, 'ere the dawn breeze stirs'. Since she knows, in the dream, that she herself is in fact imprisoned and in captivity, she realises too that harm could come to her Beloved if he remained with her. It is the opposite fantasy to that in 2:8 when she welcomed the Beloved's flight to her: now she urges him to take flight away from her, for it is too dangerous for him to remain.

She urges him to turn back, to fly away, to leap upon the mountain of Bether; that is to say, upon the mountains of division and opposition. He must fly back beyond those high and treacherous mountains that divide them in reality. It is not yet safe for him to be with her. Perhaps there is something in this fantasy that also reflects the earlier situation when her brothers' suspicions had been aroused over the secret meetings of their little sister with the Beloved.

There enters the Bride's dream yet another dramatic fantasm in verse 1 of chapter 3. The Beloved has departed; she is alone. So dramatic has been the dream experience until now that her whole being is filled with the ardour of love's desire to follow fast in flight after her departed Beloved:

> By night, upon my bed,
> I sought him whom my soul so loves;
> I sought him, but I found him not. (3:1)

This is the second time she has described her Beloved as he 'whom my *soul so loves*'. In this same dream she is to use the identical expression three more times. So it is a 'keynote' expression singing of her relationship with the beloved in a particularly intense and profound way. The word for 'my soul' – *nefeshi* – denotes the life-principle of the person. This is how she declares she loves the true Beloved – with the whole intensity of her life and being. This indicates much more a spiritual love than a physical, emotional attraction. Indeed her past, present and subsequent behaviour confirms the nobility of this deeply spiritual love-bond between her and her Beloved. It is this lofty spiritual quality of her love which imparts to her the strength to resist the King's lustful advances and to remain steadfastly faithful to her absent Beloved through all the trials yet to befall her.

Silently, another fantasy slides into her dream, and bears her off in full flight searching for her Beloved. It is only in a dream that the Bride could overreach the proprieties of sane conduct: in wakefulness she would not be seen racing alone around the streets and squares of the strange city at night to track down her Beloved. But again, her search is fruitless!

> So, now I will arise,
> I will go about the city;
> in the streets and in the squares,
> I will seek him whom my soul so loves;
> I sought him but I found him not! (3:2)

But the urgency and intensity of this flight of her love's desire urges her on still and makes her, in her dream, unafraid. Thus the watchmen patrolling the city found her. In her dream she makes bold to say to them:

> The watchmen who go about the city
> found me. (I said to them:)
> Have you seen him
> whom my soul so loves? (3:3)

She hears no reply from them, as so often there is no

reply from mere dream images. But she had scarcely passed them by when she at last found him 'whom her soul so loves'. Here again, this phenomenon is true to the principle of the soul's search for the spiritual, interior Beloved. It is not so much that he is to be found here or there, on my bed or in the city, in the streets or in the squares, or even beside the watchmen, but that he is rather to be found *only after an intensity of searching*. Her dream verifies this profound love-principle: thus it was that she found him in the dream only after that long, humiliating search – found him 'whom her soul so loves'.

It is remarkable that in this dream the Bride reiterates four times that her Beloved is the one 'whom my soul so loves'. She does not use other phrases such as 'whom I love' or 'he who loves me'. Her phrase of special choice is 'whom my soul so loves', uttered with ardent intensity. By thus bonding her love for the Beloved to her own life principle, she is saying that if the Beloved is taken away from her, denied her, then the very life principle is being torn from her breast. She has no life but in and through his love. It is this reality and conviction which will spur her on and maintain her integrity in love through all the tribulations still ahead of her before she finally comes to rest in peaceful possession of the Beloved.

The final fantasy flowing through her dream world is full of interest:

> I had scarcely passed them by
> when I found him whom my soul so loves;
> I caught hold of him,
> and would not let him go,
> until I brought him
> to my mother's house,
> even to the inner room
> of her who conceived me. (3:4)

This is the amazing dream fantasy of the young woman whom her brothers had persecuted. They would not allow her to be in any situation where she was likely to encounter 'a Beloved'. They denied her the rights of maturity. They tried to confine her and keep her as a 'little girl', as their 'little sister'.

In this dream she overrides the oppression of the siblings in her own family and as a mature woman she brings back her Beloved, to her mother's house. In fact, if we hear the fantasy aright, she brings him back to her mother's house in order to have him recognised and accepted as the one 'whom her soul so loves', and have the relationship sanctioned by her mother. By way of contrast to King Solomon's action in forcing her into his own inner room, the Bride in this dream freely brings her Beloved back, even into the inner room of her mother. This is the action of mature, open, confident love in which there is nothing to hide.

In this way, the dream of the Bride allows us to glimpse something of the maturing process of her love. We glimpse something of her maturing from adolescence to womanhood, to a healthy frankness and openness about this most intimate of all relationships. The dream also confirms the need of maturity to have this relationship acknowledged and accepted within the family circle. In this way the dream reveals the inner workings and aspirations of the Bride's heart.

Yet it is only a dream. Alas, when the dawn breeze stirs and the shadows take flight, the harsh, bitter reality of the Bride's state of captivity also dawns upon her once more with its full horror and anguish. Again she finds herself in the midst of that perplexing company of the Daughters of Jerusalem as they again take up their task of pressing her to yield to the desires of the King, their master.

Fully awake once more to these realities, the Bride turns on the Daughters of Jerusalem, reminding them

that all their efforts to cajole and incite her to respond to
the offers of spurious love from the King, are completely
in vain. She herself has already tasted the gift of authentic
love from him 'whom her soul so loves', and her recent
dream has rekindled all the desires of her heart for the
integrity of this love. It is therefore utterly useless to
imagine that she can be incited to respond to other
advances, and certainly not to the advances of a King
who is an abductor and a seducer of innocence.

> I adjure you, O Daughters of Jerusalem!
> By the hinds and gazelles of the field,
> that you do not arouse nor awaken love
> until it pleases to awake! (3:5)

The Third Song of the Bride

BYSTANDERS *(giving a description of the royal pro-*
ceedings)

3:6   What is this
         coming up from the desert,
         like columns of smoke
         perfumed with myrrh and frankincense,
         with all the merchants' aromatic powders?

3:7   Behold, it is the litter of Solomon:
         three-score mighty men surround it,
         of the mighty men of Israel.

3:8   All of them holding the sword,
         skilled in fighting,
         trained for battle;
         every man his sword
         upon his thigh,
         against the terrors in the night!

3:9   King Solomon has made
         a palanquin for himself,
         from the wood of Lebanon.

3:10   He fashioned its pillars of silver,
         its supports of gold,
         and its seat of purple;
         'twas tesselated lovingly within
         by the Daughters of Jerusalem!

3:11   Go ye forth,
         O Daughters of Zion!
         and gaze upon King Solomon

wearing the crown
with which his mother crowned him,
on his wedding day,
on the day of his heart's rejoicing!

KING SOLOMON *(arrayed in glory approaches the*
Bride)

4:1   Behold, my love,
your eyes are doves!
How fair you are,
Behold, so very fair!

Behind your veil
your hair is like
a flock of goats,
gleaming on Mount Gilead.

4:2   Your teeth are like
a flock of ewes,
newly shorn
and coming from the sheep-dip,
none of them on her own,
and all of them
perfectly paired.

4:3   Like a scarlet thread
are your lips,
and your mouth is beautiful;
like a pomegranate cut in half
are your cheeks
behind your veil!

4:4   Like the tower of David,
so is your neck
built as an armoury;
from which are hung
a thousand shields,
all the shields of the mighty men!

4:5   Your two breasts

are like two fawns,
twins of a gazelle,
delighting among the lilies!

BRIDE   *(spurning King Solomon and escaping to her*
               own quarters in the harem where she sings and
               swoons)
4:6   Ere the dawn breeze stirs,
               and the shadows take flight,
               I will hie me to the mountain of myrrh,
               and to the hill of frankincense!

(She hears her Beloved calling to her as in days of yore)

BELOVED TO HIS BRIDE *(this is the Song of the*
               Beloved)
4:7   Unblemished you are,
               and all fair, my love!
4:8   Come away from Lebanon!
               Come with me, from Lebanon!
               Come with me, my Bride!

               Depart from the peaks of Amána,
               from the crests of Senir and Mount Hermon,
               from the mountain of leopards,
               from the dens of the lion!

4:9   You have ravished my heart,
               my Sister, my Bride!
               with one glance of your eyes,
               with one link of your necklace,
               you have ravished my heart!

4:10   How fair is your love,
               my Sister, my Bride!
               How delightful your love,

more delightful than wine!
And the fragrance of your perfumes
is more fragrant than all spices!

4:11   Wild honey distils
on your lips, my Bride;
honey mingles with milk
upon your tongue!
More fragrant are your robes
than the fragrance of Lebanon!

4:12   You, my Sister, my Bride,
are a garden enclosed,
a fountain fast shut,
and a spring sealed up!

4:13   Your plants are a paradise
of pomegranate trees
with excellent fruit;
spikenard with henna,

4:14   spikenard with saffron,
calamus and cinnamon,
with every tree of frankincense;
the most select of all spices
with aloes and myrrh!

4:15   Flowing down from Lebanon,
the fountain of the gardens
is a well of living water!

BRIDE   *(responding to her Beloved in song)*
4:16   Awake! Come!
O north wind, and wind of the south,
blow upon my garden,
and the scent of its spices
will be wafted abroad!
Then let my Beloved
come into his garden,
and pluck his pleasant fruit therein!

BELOVED *(responding to the Bride in similar vein)*
5:1   I have come into my garden,
           my Sister, my Bride!
           my myrrh and my spice I have plucked!
           I have tasted my honey
           with my honeycomb,
           I have drunk my wine and my milk!

CHORUS *(probably the Daughters of Jerusalem who are
           now beginning to see the strength of the Bride's
           love for her Beloved, and to realise that she
           will not be deflected from this love)*
           Feast, O Friends!
           Drink, O Lovers, to the full!

The Third Song of the Bride (3:6–5:1)

Prologue

Bride:

> O, that he would kiss me
> with the kisses of his mouth!

> 'More delightful than wine is your love!
> Delightful, the fragrance of your perfume!'

> Your name is perfume poured out!
> That is why the maidens love you!
> Draw me after you!
> Let us make haste!
> The King has forced me
> into his rooms!

Now that the perfect Love Dream of the Second Song has faded and yielded to the harsh realities of her true situation, the desire of the Bride to be loved by her Beloved, in freedom from fear and oppression, waxes yet more ardent. The dread of what may lie ahead of her makes the integrity of authentic love an ever more desirable goal.

*   *   *

In this Third Song of the Bride, Love's Fugue now unfolds in even more dramatic tones and cadences. The counter-subject dominates the first movement (3:6–4:5). The subject is reintroduced at this point (4:6) to be followed by a superb treatment of the real answer throughout the remainder of the song (4:7–5:1). In this song the concluding chorus differs from the earlier choruses.

We can briefly tabulate the three movements of this song as:

(a) the counter-subject (the King Solomon scene, 3:6–4:5);
(b) the subject (the Bride's reaction, 4:6);
(c) the real answer (the Beloved's song and scene, 4:7–5:1);
(d) chorus (5:1c).

The counter-subject: the King Solomon scene (3:6–4:5)

This movement of the song has two divisions. In verses 3:6–11 the bystanders observe what is happening and sing a description of the events. From 4:1–5 King Solomon sings his song.

The bystanders' commentary (3:6–11)
The unnamed bystanders begin with a question which immediately brings us into the picture of what is taking place:

What is this
coming up from the desert,
like columns of smoke
perfumed with myrrh and frankincense,
with all the merchants' aromatic powders? (3:6)

What can this procession be with its clouds and columns of smoke billowing out before it, spreading around its luxurious perfumes? It seems to be advancing towards them in all its splendour and majesty. No wonder their curiosity is aroused and they borrow words reminiscent of the pillar of cloud recalling the presence of God guiding his people from slavery to freedom through the desert. No wonder we feel our own curiosity being aroused and then heightened as we join in to gaze on this amazing desert procession.

The reply which the bystanders give to their own question brings us back to reality. What we behold is not a vision of divine and holy splendour but a procession of worldly pomp and power.

> Behold, it is the litter of Solomon:
> three-score mighty men surround it,
> of the mighty men of Israel.
> All of them holding the sword,
> skilled in fighting,
> trained for battle;
> every man his sword
> upon his thigh,
> against the terrors in the night! (3:7,8)

Here comes King Solomon's litter surrounded by heavily armed skilled fighting men, each with his sword at the ready, against the terrors of the night. So it is an evening or night scene.

We are all familiar with the image of the petty tyrant or dictator who surrounds himself with his armed henchmen when he is about to strike or make the coup which will bring him into his ambitious, ego-boosting position of power. We know with equal certainty, that lurking behind such despots and their henchmen there is always the fear, dread and even hidden terror at what may unexpectedly befall.

The heavily armed henchmen of King Solomon are meant to impress, overawe and perhaps intimidate the Bride. But the display of warlike grandeur is a further revelation to her that King Solomon's intentions in her regard are decidedly on the level of power, coercion, domination and lust. Authentic love, or anything remotely worthy of that name, is quite foreign to him.

Perhaps the Bride questions *why* the King, together with his armed men, is so afraid of the night? What terrors does it hold for them?

The climax of this procession of power is the view of King Solomon reclining in his palanquin. The description of this so-called 'litter', by the bystanders, is simply another demonstration of worldly pomp and power:

> King Solomon has made
> a palanquin for himself,
> from the wood of Lebanon.
> He fashioned its pillars of silver,
> its supports of gold,
> and its seat of purple;
> 'twas tesselated lovingly within
> by the Daughters of Jerusalem! (3:9,10)

Fashioned of the finest wood of Lebanon with pillars of silver, supports of gold, its couch of richest purple and the whole cunningly decorated within by the King's women servants, it was indeed a palanquin fit for royalty! But what is the purpose of this particular display of regal splendour and kingly power? The answer to this question comes in verse 11:

> Go ye forth,
> O Daughters of Zion!
> and gaze upon King Solomon
> wearing the crown
> with which his mother crowned him,
> on his wedding day,
> on the day of his heart's rejoicing!

In this scene the Bride, the Shulamitess, is perhaps one among these 'Daughters of Zion', invited to go forth to meet the King. It is a scene indelibly imprinted on her imagination, for the King's gorgeous apparel is certainly a sign of his intent. He is crowned as he had been by his mother on his wedding day. So the Daughters of Zion are not mistaken in believing that this present grandiose display is the sign of his intent to proceed to yet another form of marriage. He already has many wives. Is it now his intent to dazzle yet another Daughter of Zion and ensnare her into becoming another victim of his lustful alliances?

By now the Bride, the Shulamitess, has sufficient experience of life in the King's harem, and is instinctively on her guard. Grandiose ritual or not, she will have no part in it. Caught up unwillingly in a situation beyond her control, she has already learnt to resist involvement and remain aloof from the situation.

But it is upon her that the King casts his eye and directs the full flood of his seductive flattery.

King Solomon's song to the Shulamitess the Bride (4:1–5)

The first five verses of the King's song to the Bride (Shulamitess) form a mounting tide of flattery. One peculiar characteristic of this song is that King Solomon takes up his flattery at the very point where he had left off in his earlier song (1:15), and using that as his point of departure builds up his flattering assault of the Bride:

> Behold, my love,
> your eyes are doves!
> How fair you are,
> behold, so very fair! (4:1; 1:15)

Then the royal flattery proceeds step by step, enumerating the physical details of the Shulamitess. While the fashion of the East in love songs tends to be more 'bodily' in expression than is generally acceptable in the West, we should not be deluded into thinking that the King's song is an authentic love song expressing his true feelings towards the Shulamitess. The compliments fall readily from his lips as being a long-practised art, as he dwells one by one on her physical charms in order to arouse in her a physical response.

As we listen to his words we need to be ever aware that she has become an object of his seductive advances because his relationship with her rests upon his original action in abducting her and then forcing her into his harem (1:4b). The initial act of violence and coercion necessarily colours all his subsequent words and actions.

Not one aspect of her physical appearance remains untouched. Her eyes, hair, teeth, lips, mouth, cheeks, neck and breasts all receive equal attention from him.

> Behold, my love,
> your eyes are doves! (4:1a)

Perhaps the gentleness, meekness and tenderness of doves are what he seeks to convey by this comparison. We need to remember this specific compliment, for later on, in the Fifth Song, he will change his mind about her eyes and the effect that they have on him.

He moves on to extol the gleaming, flowing quality of her jet-black hair:

> Behind your veil
> your hair is like
> a flock of goats,
> gleaming on Mount Gilead. (4:1)

The image here is powerful and emotive. It recalls for the Bride, who is just a simple country shepherdess, the rugged rural scene set in the region beyond the Jordan, of a flock of black goats streaming down Mount Gilead being taken out to pasture. The dawning sun catches their lithe movement down the mountainside, their coats shining and gleaming as they pass before their shepherd or shepherdess. Just so, the luxurious hair of the Shulamitess waves, gleams and flows down her shoulders.

Perhaps King Solomon's choice of Mount Gilead as this particular point of comparison with the Bride contains a scarcely concealed touch of the cynicism that betrays his true intent in all this flattery, for Gilead means hard, harsh, rough. Are these the real characteristics of the seducer himself? Or is he beginning to find, in spite of his smooth words and sophisticated song, that the Shulamitess is in fact far harder and tougher than he thought in her resistance to him?

He pursues the shepherd imagery familiar to the captive Shulamitess. He progresses to his description of the pearly white evenness of her teeth, so evenly matched as they are, and compares them to the clean whiteness of newly shorn sheep emerging in pairs from their cleansing in the sheep dip:

> Your teeth are like
> a flock of ewes,
> newly shorn
> and coming from the sheep-dip,
> none of them on her own,
> and all of them
> perfectly paired. (4:2)

Apart from this evocative imagery about the gleaming smile of the Bride revealing the perfection of her teeth, do we detect here a subtle gleam of Solomon's own tenacity in courting this maid? Is he deliberately evoking, in her, the memory of that great wooer of women, Jacob, who astutely outwitted his father-in-law, Laban, when the latter deceived him over the bride-price for one and then two of his daughters? To gain both Rachel and Leah, along with his own freedom, Jacob bargained with Laban setting the condition for his wages in terms of the colour and number of the sheep he was breeding. Aided by God, Jacob bred the sheep he had agreed for his side of the bargain in such a way as to ensure he had the best of the deal. By setting striped and mottled branches before them as they mated at their watering troughs he was able to influence the breeding to his own advantage (Genesis 29–31).

In his continued efforts to tempt and arouse a response in the Shulamitess, is King Solomon craftily equating his own techniques to those which Jacob used?

In 4:3 the King concentrates on the lovely face of the Shulamitess:

> Like a scarlet thread
> are your lips,
> and your mouth is beautiful;
> like a pomegranate cut in half
> are your cheeks
> behind your veil! (4:3)

It is a tantalising description calculated to please most women. Sure of himself the King hastens on to his next flattering portrayal of the beauty of this girl whom he is confident will soon yield to him and go through the form of a mock wedding with him:

> Like the tower of David,
> so is your neck
> built as an armoury;
> from which are hung
> a thousand shields,
> all the shields of the mighty men! (4:4)

A cursory glance at this poetic flight does not immediately enable us to see that it is in fact a rather curious turn of phrase. The young girl's finely shaped neck is held high and carries the immense weight of the 'gold collars, silver studded shields' which the King himself has promised to give her. Certainly not a very comfortable style of jewellery, even in his circles!

Given the situation of this mock wedding procession, and the earlier remarks of the bystanders, we are led to look more deeply into this figure of speech used deliberately by the King.

The bystanders have proclaimed the King's processional approach in his royal litter in terms of the advance of a king surrounded by three-score mighty men, armed to the teeth, swords in hand, skilled in fighting, trained for battle – well prepared against the terrors of the night!

Now, in his song, the King approaches the Shulamitess adorned with the rich variety of jewels and gems given to her by himself. He proclaims her appearance by comparing it to another king's armoury, and to the tall turret or tower of David, hung with a thousand shields of all the fighting men!

This figure of speech increases the strangeness of the scene. It is more like a military confrontation than a mock courting scene, although the setting seems to be the 'wasf' or procession with ritual sword-dance included in oriental wedding ceremonies.

On the one hand, King Solomon gorgeously arrayed is surrounded by his sixty mighty men all with their sharpened swords on the offensive. On the other, there is this lone, rustic maid, dressed up in the King's luxurious clothes, and weighed down by her heavy collars of gold studded with silver, like an armoury wall well lined with stout shields. The King and his men are in fact bent on an act of aggression and violation of her womanly dignity. The simple maid is evidently strongly on the defensive: she is behind the array of impenetrable shields, not of King David, nor of the 'mighty men', but of her own chastity and resolute fidelity to her true Beloved, albeit absent and invisible.

The King therefore seems to acknowledge this impasse, by using this extraordinary image of tower, armoury and shields to indicate the virtue of this intractable maiden.

Despite the fact that she remains implacable, impenetrable, the King launches one last offensive in his lustful strategy. Her heavy ornaments, suspended from her neck and lying on her bosom, lead him on:

> Your two breasts
> are like two fawns,
> twins of a gazelle,
> delighting among the lilies! (4:5)

He has missed his mark. The Bride's reaction convinces us of this.

The subject: the Bride's reaction (4:6)

The Bride Shulamitess now takes up her own song, returning to the theme she had used earlier in 2:17 where she had urged her true Beloved to come to her rescue. Now she dramatically and impetuously makes clear her desire to be free from the evil prince of power. She must flee, immediately. Even though it is impossible she must flee and make it clear that she will have no part in this sham wedding ceremony:

> Ere the dawn breeze stirs,
> and the shadows take flight,
> I will hie me to the mountain of myrrh,
> and to the hill of frankincense! (4:6)

While she sings she retreats quickly back into the crowd of Daughters of Zion and the bystanders, impelled by the sheer force of her emotional revulsion against the King. To flee away and find her true Beloved is her only desire.

Perhaps she collapses and swoons from sheer emotional prostration, and has to be carried back to the harem by the Daughters of Jerusalem. We do not know. But she has made her point, dramatically and plainly. She must flee from this situation.

Attended by the Daughters of Jerusalem who are trying to revive her, she launches into a description of the Song of True Love, sung to her long ago by her true Beloved. It is this song, this real answer to the theme of her love's desire, that we now hear as the text continues to unfold. It is a kind of compensatory interlude called forth by the cruel drama of the actual situation of the Shulamitess.

The real answer: the Beloved's song and scene (4:7–5:1)

The song which the Beloved now sings to the Bride is radically different. Whereas the King's song launched a direct and detailed assault on the physical beauty of the Bride which strikes us as quite offensive, the Song of the Beloved is more general in its compliments, more finely poetic in its figures of speech, and more genuinely revealing of his attitude of deep reverence towards the Bride and their relationship.

In his opening words he seems to be reassuring the Bride that he knows she has not sullied her purity even though she has been taken captive in the King's harem and has been the object of his lustful advances. The Beloved describes the Bride as being not only beautiful, but also unblemished:

> Unblemished you are,
> and all fair, my love! (4:7)

Whereas King Solomon had proceeded to detail and linger over each physical charm of the Bride, the Beloved once more shows that he knows that the Bride needs more than anything else to come away from the place of coercion and captivity:

> Come away from Lebanon!
> Come with me, from Lebanon!
> Come with me, my Bride!

> Depart from the peaks of Amána,
> from the crests of Senir and Mount Hermon,
> from the mountain of leopards,
> from the dens of the lion! (4:8)

The Beloved, though absent, perceives her situation. He is not content with urging and pleading with her to come away with him. His plea also respects her freedom. Unlike Solomon, he will not force her to come with him. While he grasps her predicament, he also indicates that she herself must choose to take the initiative, and come away from the King's harem and Mount Lebanon.

He reinforces his invitation with words of deep comfort – she is to come *with him*, for she and she alone is his Bride. He does not speak of armed or mighty men to help in this flight from the King. For him it is a more fundamental question – the choice to come away has to be made with whatever freedom can be mustered.

As yet, the Beloved clearly sees that the Bride is unblemished, but he feels it his place to speak frankly about the grave situation in which she is held captive. 'Depart,' he urges her, 'from that residence of Solomon on the fortified peaks of Lebanon, for that place is nothing but the dwelling-place of wild beasts, with Solomon the most treacherous of them all. It is the place of leopards, the lair of Solomon and the den of the lion – the place of his cohabitation with the victims of lust, his prey.'

The Beloved will never force her to depart. He will not come and carry her off physically. His part is to urge her to come away. It is for her, and her alone, to respond to the invitation and come away, depart from the danger. While it appears that she is irreversibly trapped and ensnared, the Beloved reminds her that she still has it in her power to free herself. Is she not still unblemished? Is she not in truth his own Bride?

The remainder of his song reiterates this with the greatest trust and tenderness. It is a term King Solomon never used in her regard, nor could he. Her Beloved alone can call her 'Bride'. Five times he uses this crucial term in the song he is singing to her – 'my Bride' (4:8,9,10,11,12); my unblemished *Bride*.

No greater reassurance or encouragement could be offered to the trapped girl than these two words on the lips of her Beloved. To this term he links another word of endearment which King Solomon would never have the audacity to use: 'my *Sister*, my Bride' (4:9,10,12).

But the Beloved, in using terms of the most profound tenderness and clearest honesty with the Bride, proceeds in a manner totally contrary to the style of King Solomon. His blandishments itemise in close detail each bodily aspect of the Bride, yet never once does he exhibit any feeling of genuine tenderness for her. The Beloved, on the other hand, reveals *his own* delight in and response to the Bride in a way that everyone can find acceptable:

> You have ravished my heart,
> my Sister, my Bride!
> with one glance of your eyes,
> with one link of your necklace,
> you have ravished my heart! (4:9)

There is noble sentiment here, not seductive flattery. The Beloved reiterates his own inner, personal response to the Bride's merest glance, to the least link in her original necklace of beads – in the presence of these his heart is completely ravished.

He waxes lyrical, not over the mere physical beauty and perfection of the Bride as did King Solomon, but over the rare quality of her love for him, over its pure and thrilling power over him. In so doing he reveals himself to be her authentic Beloved, for he sings of her love in the identical terms which she herself recalled in 1:2–3:

> How fair is your love,
> my Sister, my Bride!
> How delightful your love,
> more delightful than wine! (4:10)

Like mellow wine, her love also has its special fragrance and he stumbles, stammering out words to describe it:

> And the fragrance of your perfumes,
> is more fragrant than all spices! (4:10)

The alluring sweetness of her love and the fragrant garden of her personality are qualities over which he lingers. He links them to the overflowing richness and goodness of her words and conversation. He eulogises both her speech and her personality in richly evocative imagery:

> Wild honey distils
> on your lips, my Bride;
> honey mingles with milk
> upon your tongue!
> More fragrant are your robes
> than the fragrance of Lebanon! (4:11)

The phrase 'the fragrance of Lebanon' contains a twofold meaning. The first is that as Lebanon was famous for its fragrant perfume, his Bride is yet more fragrant. The second is that in the context of this song he calls her to 'come away and depart from Lebanon' because it is a treacherous place, and he is telling her that her fragrance is much more enticing than the odorous heaviness of the lion's lair where she is captive at this moment. Her fragrance is rare, exotic and well-pleasing in comparison with the smell exuding from the Lebanon of King Solomon's harem.

As further encouragement to her, the Beloved continues to reiterate that in comparison to the kind of activity carried on in King Solomon's harem, the Bride's condition is one of the clearest virtue, integrity and inviolate purity:

> You, my Sister, my Bride,
> are a garden enclosed,
> a fountain fast shut,
> and a spring sealed up! (4:12)

This figure of speech on the lips of the Beloved extols not only the Bride's virginity but also establishes definitively his own relationship to her. Her modesty and chastity are like a garden walled in and enclosed, against the wrongful intrusion of all strangers. The garden enclosed, shut against all unlawful intruders, is the sole possession of its lawful owner – her Beloved.

The fountain fast shut and the spring sealed up convey the same message in the traditional fashion of the oriental practice of fountain owners sealing their fountains with clay which quickly hardened in the hot sun, so making the fountain yet more strictly the private property of the owner alone. When he wills he unlocks the fountain and it plays; he unstops the spring, and it flows. The Bride is the strictly private property of the Beloved. She is his garden, his fountain, and his alone.

The Beloved now passes on to an even more lyrical description of the beauties and pleasures of his garden – his Bride. It is an outpouring of the finest sensitivity, exquisitely relating the delights of their relationship:

> Your plants are a paradise
> of pomegranate trees
> with excellent fruit;
> spikenard with henna,
> spikenard with saffron,
> calamus and cinnamon,
> with every tree of frankincense;
> the most select of all spices
> with aloes and myrrh!
>
> Flowing down from Lebanon,
> the fountain of the gardens
> is a well of living water! (4:13–15)

This profusion of rare and precious fruits and spices proliferating in the garden which is his Bride highlights the rarity yet abundance of her virtue and charm. All this is carefully cultivated for the Beloved alone. The marvellous array of pleasant fruitfulness is plentifully watered and made more fruitful by the living fountain flowing down from the heights of Mount Lebanon. Pomegranates, spikenard, henna, saffron, calamus, cinnamon, frankincense trees, select spices, aloes and myrrh, many of which came from India and other distant, eastern lands to Palestine, were greatly prized for their fragrant oils or used as aromatic herbs. All this wealth, richness and variety of virtue luxuriate in the person of the Bride.

The fountain fast shut is the spring sealed up of verse 12 which is shut only to outsiders. Within the garden it flows abundantly, forming in the midst of the trees, plants and herbs a deep well of living water, symbolising the stillness, peace, fecundity and constancy of the Bride's love for her Beloved. It is a love kept only for him, and for no other. Only he has the right to enter this garden and take his delight therein.

Her Beloved's song, which began with its urgent invitation to come away, to depart from the dire peril of her present situation, continued to reassure and encourage her so that she now replies to him gladly and freely with her invitation issued in the same terms as those of his song to her.

It would be unthinkable for the Bride to treat her Beloved as she had treated King Solomon by spurning him and seeking to flee away. No: the free mutuality and wealth of love between the Bride and the Beloved is taken up into the song of her responsive invitation to him. In her turn she rises to an equal wealth of imagery, matching everything sung of her by the Beloved, acknowledging with modesty that she is *his* garden, and that he alone has the right to the abundant fruit thereof:

> Awake! Come!
> O north wind, and wind of the south,
> blow upon my garden,
> and the scent of its spices
> will be wafted abroad!
> Then let my Beloved
> come into his garden,
> and pluck his pleasant fruit therein! (4:16)

Here the Bride invites the winds and breezes from both north and south to blow through her garden so that by stirring up and wafting abroad the rich variety of fragrances from herbs and flowers, her Beloved will be enchanted and delighted when he comes into what is his garden.

Again, this image is entirely devoid of any force, violence or coercion. It is couched in terms of mutual reverence and confidence. She speaks in one breath of *my* garden, and in the next of *his* garden, the garden of the Beloved. Nor does she even invite him directly to come into her garden. She is content to sing 'Let him come', if he will; but I am ready for his coming. Let him come and pluck his pleasant fruit in the garden. Her words seem almost casual. They are words welling up from the deep intimacy between herself and her Beloved, an intimacy that is founded on mutual confidence that nothing can shake. Their relationship is so deep, pure and true that, confident in his love for her, a direct invitation is not needed. She is neither dilatory nor presumptuous in letting him know that her garden is his garden and that he is free to come into it. Their mutuality in love is complete and trustful. She is confident that now she is ready and open to his coming, that he will indeed come unhindered.

The Beloved responds, fulfilling all the Bride's desires for him to come into the garden:

> I have come into my garden,
> my Sister, my Bride!
> my myrrh and my spice I have plucked!
> I have tasted my honey
> with my honeycomb,
> I have drunk my wine and my milk! (5:1)

The Beloved's words draw together with the finest delicacy all the preceding imagery of his song. Thus we are left with the delightful scene of the Beloved with his Bride/Sister enjoying in untrammelled freedom their intimate converse and mutual exchange of love in the privacy of *his* garden to which she has given him free access.

In the way the Beloved designates his activity in his garden – plucking *my* myrrh, *my* spice, of tasting *my* honey, *my* honeycomb, of drinking *my* wine and *my* milk – we understand that he is figuratively redrawing his portrait of the Bride which he has already painted so vividly in verses 4:10–15. But this time he does it with an even greater refinement of love and tenderness and that complete assurance that she, and she alone, is truly '*my* Sister, *my* Bride'.

This brief glimpse into the nobility and totality of the mutual love between the Bride and the Beloved introduces to the Daughters of Jerusalem who attend her, a world of purity, integrity, mutual reverence in a relationship that makes them gasp in amazement at a truth and goodness quite foreign to their experience of life. Her impetuous flight from King Solomon ended in a swoon and as they tried to revive her in order to re-present her to the King so that he could continue the mock wedding ritual, they found themselves taken off-guard, astonished and full of a sense of wonder they thought to have long since outgrown. Something of respect for truth and integrity sparks within them and they cry out their comment on the revelation of love the Bride has just given them:

> Feast, O Friends!
> Drink, O Lovers, to the full! (5:1)

Thus their contact with the Bride is beginning to cause them to change their allegiance, in spite of themselves, and they take this one step out of the camp of lust towards the tent of love.

The Bride even in the darkest hour of temptation still has resources of freedom and strength which enable her to escape the advance of evil. The eternal Beloved also remains free to make inner spiritual visitations to the Bride as and when he will. And even the worldly-wise, when they occasionally glimpse this working of love's true integrity, cry out in congratulation.

The Fourth Song of the Bride

BRIDE   *(singing in her fitful sleep. Her Beloved calls to*
          her and she replies)

5:2   I slumber, but my heart is watching.
          Hark! My Beloved is knocking!
          'Open! Open to me, my Sister!
          My love, my dove, my perfect one!
          For my head is drenched with dew,
          the locks of my hair
          with the dew-drops of the night!'

5:3   'I have taken off my garment,
          how could I put it on again?
          I have bathed my feet,
          how could I soil them once more?'

5:4   My Beloved thrust his hand
          through the hole of the door,
          and my heart then sighed for him.

5:5   I arose to open to my Beloved,
          my hands were moist with myrrh,
          my fingers were dripping myrrh
          upon the bolt of the door.

5:6   I opened the door to my Beloved:
          but he had departed;
          my Beloved had passed me by.
          My soul swooned away
          at the sound of his singing.
          I searched for him,
          but I found him not;

I called to him,
but he answered me not.

5:7   The watchmen patrolling the city
found me; they took away my mantle,
they smote me, they wounded me –
those watchers of the walls!

5:8   I adjure you, O Daughters of Jerusalem,
if you should find my Beloved,
what message will you give him?
– That I am wounded with love!

DAUGHTERS OF JERUSALEM *(replying to the Bride)*
5:9   Who is your Beloved,
O fairest of women?
Who is your Beloved
to be loved above all others,
that you should adjure us so?

BRIDE   *(to the Daughters of Jerusalem, describing the
beauty of her Beloved)*
5:10   My Beloved's complexion
is radiant and ruddy;
my Beloved is like a banner unfurled
in the midst of ten thousand!

5:11   His head is like finest gold;
his locks are wavy,
and black as a raven.

5:12   His eyes are pleasingly placed,
like doves washed with milk
beside the water brooks.

5:13   His cheeks are like spices,
like banks of aromatic herbs;
his lips are like lilies
distilling liquid myrrh.

5:14	His hands are like circlets of gold
	embedded with beryl;
	overlaid with sapphires
	his torso is ivory
	polished and smooth.
5:15	His limbs are columns of marble
	set upon sockets of finest gold;
	and his bearing is like Lebanon,
	stately as its cedars.

5:16   His speech is gracious,
        and he is wholly desirable.
        This is my Beloved,
        and this is my lover.
        O ye Daughters of Jerusalem!

DAUGHTERS OF JERUSALEM *(to the Bride, and
        showing perhaps just too much interest in her
        Beloved)*
6:1   Whither has he gone, your Beloved,
        O fairest of women?
        Whither has your Beloved turned aside?
        That with you we may search for him!

BRIDE   *(regretting somewhat that she has spoken so
        freely of her Beloved, and reaffirming that her
        Beloved is hers alone)*
6:2   My Beloved is gone
        down into his garden,
        unto the banks of spices;
        gleaning the lilies,
        in the gardens taking his delight.

6:3   My Beloved is mine,
        and I am his:
        among the lilies
        he takes his delight!

The Fourth Song of the Bride (5:2–6:3)

Prologue

Bride:

> O, that he would kiss me
> with the kisses of his mouth!

> 'More delightful than wine is your love!
> Delightful, the fragrance of your perfume!'

> Your name is perfume poured out!
> That is why the maidens love you!
> Draw me after you!
> Let us make haste!
> The King has forced me
> into his rooms!

This Prologue to the entire Love's Fugue again finds its fitting place at the beginning of yet another of the individual songs, replete as it is with the Bride's concise summing-up of her situation as well as her ecstatic desire and longing for her Beloved to comfort her with his presence and reassure her that her desire to be loved is not in vain.

*   *   *

The drama and highly charged emotion of the Third Song of the Bride yield once more to a troubled, restless sleep for the remainder of this eventful night. Disturbing dreams slide through her mind as delightful and tortured fantasma, strung together by the nonsensical, disjointed actions and attitudes that are possible only in the world of dreams. The Daughters of Jerusalem, still in attendance on the Bride, are like so many half-willing eavesdroppers who thus learn more about the Bride and her Beloved. Once the Bride is fully awake they question her more closely about her Beloved, and a conversation takes place between the Bride and these worldly women.

So the Fourth Song of the Bride falls naturally into two main movements, both of which provide a rather different treatment of the main subject: the Bride's desire to be loved, and the real answer of the love of the Beloved for the Bride. The two movements can be delineated thus:

1. The disturbed and disturbing dream of the Bride (5:2–8):
   (a) the jumbled dream of desire and indecision (5:2–3)
   (b) her dream about the Beloved and the Bride's passive, then active, response (5:4–6)
   (c) the twofold wounding of the Bride (5:7–8).
2. The conversation with the Daughters of Jerusalem (5:9–6:3):
   (a) the questions of the Daughters of Jerusalem (5:9)
   (b) the Bride's reply (5:10–16)
   (c) the curiosity of the Daughters of Jerusalem (6:1)
   (d) the Bride's jealousy (6:2–3).

The disturbed and disturbing dream of the Bride (5:2–8)

The jumbled dream of desire and indecision (5:2–3)

The keynote on which the dream opens is that of the intense desire of the Bride for her Beloved. Even sleep cannot obliterate the ardent movement of her desire to be loved by him:

> I slumber, but my heart is watching.
> Hark! My Beloved is knocking! (5:2a)

Thus she hears the Beloved calling and knocking on the door, seeking admittance. As he continues knocking and calling, the Bride, in the strange bondage of sleep, savours the delight of his coming to her. But although the delight of his coming is so vivid in her dream, she continues to cling to her dream slumber, seeming to ignore his knocking and his desire to come in to her. Yet he still knocks and calls to her more urgently:

> Open! Open to me, my Sister!
> My love, my dove, my perfect one!
> For my head is drenched with dew,
> the locks of my hair
> with the dew-drops of the night! (5:2b,c,d)

In his dramatic search and desire for his lost, abducted Bride, the Beloved has not spared himself any trouble or exhaustion for her sake. He has searched alone and unaided, even in the dark and peril of the night until he is weary and his hair is drenched with the abundance of dew peculiar to the cold, desert nights in the East.

His call to the Bride is couched not only in terms of his ardent desire to be with her, but also in terms of his own personal need – to leave behind and outside the fatiguing, cramping night search and the chilling dampness of the dew. Now that he has finally located the Bride, he does not question that she will welcome him and draw him in out of the cold dark night, to be with her in the warmth of her room. He continues to knock and to call, almost to plead with her to let him in . . .

In this again how different is the Beloved from King Solomon. The Beloved expends all his virile, youthful vigour in discovering the place to which the Bride has been carried by her captor. But once he has arrived there after a long and arduous search, he will use no force to take her for his own. Instead, he meekly and humbly begs and pleads with her to give him entrance to her. He is prepared to use his own wet and weary condition as an added persuasion, when he meets with a delay in her response. But he leaves the consent to her: it must be her choice. Meanwhile he waits outside in the cold and in the dark.

At this critical moment in her dream the Bride seems to waver and hesitate, in an indecision that appears inexplicable. Instead of freely and eagerly opening the door or window to her Beloved with the alacrity of love, she trembles with indecision: a momentary indecision for which she is to pay dearly.

Her reply is heard, coming back to him from some dark part of her being, previously hidden from her own awareness; from a part of her not yet fully purified by love's ardour. It is only in a dream that she could have the initial confrontation with this dark corner of her personality, and could in her waking awareness, strive to accept this weakness and counter it with greater humility and integrity. How quickly the finely sensitive edge of her love's desire has become blunted by the comforts and material security of life in the King's harem.

In this disturbing dream she learns that lurking within her heart is this tendency towards personal comfort and material security. It is a horrifying truth that this makes her sluggish in risking inconvenience, even for her Beloved. Until now, this core of self-centredness has been veiled from her self-knowledge, falling behind her, out of sight, like her shadow.

Almost before she realises what is happening, this lack

of true self-perception receives its proper expression in
her dream as she replies to the knocking of the Beloved:

> I have taken off my garment,
> how could I put it on again?
> I have bathed my feet,
> how could I soil them once more? (5:3)

Even as she voices the words she is appalled at what they
reveal to her of herself. It is this shock which brings her
to her senses. In that terrible moment she passes from
immaturity in love as a maiden to maturity in love as
a woman. The hitherto unknown core of egoism and
selfishness in her personality is now recognised. From
now on she will reckon with this weakness in herself
and will constantly seek to counter its downward pull
by her free, determined choice of love and self-sacrifice
for the good of her Beloved. His desires and needs will
henceforth be her priority in life. No longer will she simply
desire to be loved by him, but will sacrifice everything in
herself to offer him the love he seeks from her.

She learns this imperative lesson about love, and is
purified and matured by it, in the disturbing crucible of
this second love-dream. Her future actions reveal that it
has been a purifying lesson fully and powerfully learnt.
But for the moment, her dream flows on disturbingly.

Her dream of the Beloved and the Bride's passive, then active, response (5:4–6)

The Beloved, however, nothing daunted, resorts to another
way of expressing his desire for the Bride. He ceases
knocking and thrusts his hand through the hole in the
door, near the door-bolt. (According to the custom of
the East, this hole in the door enabled the door to be
opened from the inside while the person was standing on
the outside.) Thus he shows the Bride that he could have

unlocked the latch and entered. But thus far he goes, and
no farther:

> My Beloved thrust his hand
> through the hole of the door . . .(5:4)

The Bride's reaction to the Beloved's new approach swings
from paralysing passivity to electrifying action:

> and my heart then sighed for him. (5:4)

She remains still, trembling on her bed, inwardly thrilling
and sighing at his closeness and coming to her; but he does
not enter. Galvanised then into action in her dream:

> I arose to open to my Beloved,
> my hands were moist with myrrh,
> my fingers were dripping myrrh
> upon the bolt of the door.
> I opened the door to my Beloved:
> but he had departed;
> my Beloved had passed me by.(5:5–6)

The feverish pitch of her activity and the certainty that
her Beloved is at the door, takes the Bride completely off
guard and stuns her when she finds on opening the door
that he has gone; he has passed her by, inexplicably!

In dreams much is inexplicable, yet much can be learnt.
The Bride learns instantly what is still needful to her for
the perfecting of her own love response to the Beloved.
Her immediate reaction is dramatic and anguished:

> My soul swooned away
> at the sound of his singing. (5:6)

The impossible has happened. Her Beloved, her own
Beloved, has actually come so close to her and yet

passed her by! His voice can still be heard growing fainter and fainter in the distance. From shock and grief she swoons.

Has she been careless in her dream, lacking in vigilance in her emotional self-absorption? Is this attitude somehow similar to her earlier situation back in her brothers' vineyard when she was taken off-guard and snatched away by King Solomon's henchmen?

The dream has been horrifyingly clear. It is teaching her the same lesson as the one sung to her by the Beloved (4:8) in kinder yet equally clear words:

> Come away from Lebanon!
> Depart . . . from the dens of the lion. (4:8)

'Come away – depart – or you too will be contaminated in some way by association with evil. Even though you are captive – come away! Depart.'

Her Beloved had been teaching her essential lessons about the integrity of love, and she had only dimly perceived it. He was then teaching her with much gentleness the lesson that this dream now teaches sharply, shaking her into stark reality. The essential lesson of love's integrity is about free, constant and responsible choice.

She had thought herself totally trapped in the clutches of the King, and so had relied on her Beloved somehow to do the impossible and set her free again. True, she yearned for him and desired him with all her heart. Equally, she had consistently spurned the lustful advances of the King and repeatedly fled from him to the relative safety of the women's quarters in his harem. But until now she had accepted passively the impossibility of actually escaping from her present predicament. In fact she had trusted that one day – or one night – her Beloved would himself come and set her free. This was her desire and her constant preoccupation.

But this dream is telling her something else. Her Beloved will come – he himself will take her away into freedom from the King. But his coming with his power and his intent to save her are not enough. She must freely arise from sleep and come away with him. In other words, she has the responsibility of choosing to escape, and she must be willing to escape from the domination of the King. She has the power to choose this – the transforming power of the love of her Beloved for his chosen one. If she does not rise and make this choice she may find that her Beloved has come and has passed her by, never to return.

It is a sobering realisation; the more so when she adds it to the lesson learnt a verse or so earlier – namely that she is actually finding some aspects of life in the King's harem rather comfortable. This comfort too she must make the object of her deliberate choice in order to depart from it, to seek her Beloved in his simple, rustic way of life.

The consequences of this new awakening within her dream are clear and decisive for the Bride.

The twofold wounding of the Bride (5:6b–8)

Once the numbing fog of her dream swoon has dissolved, a new fortitude and determination strengthen her resolve, and her new-found fortitude and determination are tested severely and immediately. The test comes in the form of the keenest disappointment for her:

> I searched for him,
> but I found him not;
> I called to him,
> but he answered me not.

> The watchmen patrolling the city
> found me; they took away my mantle,
> they smote me, they wounded me –
> those watchers of the walls! (5:6b–7)

The Bride in her dream exerts all her energies to depart from her room, in search of her Beloved. Every effort proves futile and useless. The very fruitlessness of her search spurs her on to ever greater efforts. In her desperate search throughout the city the night patrol finds her and shows a completely different attitude from that of her former dream in a similar situation (3:2,3). In this nightmarish dream the nightwatchers treat her harshly, beat her up and wound her cruelly for her trouble!

But the Bride's new-found fortitude and determination do not desert her in these dire straits. In her tortured dream she takes a yet more daring step in her search for the Beloved. She turns, wounded though she is, and seeks help from those who are officially on the side of the seducer, King Solomon.

Perhaps in her dream memory she recalls their beginnings of approval and appreciation of her relationship with her Beloved. She remembers that at the conclusion of the Beloved's song to her, recently, they had burst out:

> Feast, O Friends!
> Drink, O Lovers, to the full! (5:1c)

So now, on the knife-edge of despair, she risks turning to them for help in the one thing that is absolutely imperative for her at this moment – the finding of the Beloved. So she takes the plunge, and hazards the attempt to win them more fully to her cause:

> I adjure you, O Daughters of Jerusalem,
> if you should find my Beloved,
> what message will you give him?
> – That I am wounded with love! (5:8)

The anguished resolution implied in this turning to the Daughters of Jerusalem shakes the Bride out of the residue of her dream, and, barely awake, she hears the women responding in reality to her exhausted plea. They had remained near her throughout the night, and had caught snatches of her troubled dream. Here they are now, at her side, replying to her in unison:

> Who is your Beloved,
> O fairest of women?
> Who is your Beloved
> to be loved above all others,
> that you should adjure us so? (5:9)

This is indeed a different side to the Daughters of Jerusalem. Here they are, to all intents and purposes showing themselves to be her allies.

This is also the opportunity for which the Bride has been yearning for some time, to help assuage that now twofold wounding of love; her chance to sing the full praises of her Beloved unhampered by the usual cynicism and sarcasm of the worldly women of the harem, especially the Daughters of Jerusalem.

The conversation with the Daughters of Jerusalem (5:9–6:3)

The questions of the Daughters of Jerusalem (5:9)

Let us take another look at the questions posed to the Bride by the Daughters of Jerusalem:

> Who is your Beloved,
> O fairest of women?
> Who is your Beloved
> to be loved above all others,
> that you should adjure us so? (5:9)

It is difficult to know just how sincere are these questions of the Daughters of Jerusalem. Are they being genuinely converted to favour the Bride? Is the increasing contact with her and her talk of her Beloved really making some genuine impact on them and their way of thinking? Or are they merely occupying themselves with a novel kind of plaything to while away the time? Is there still some lingering sincerity in their worldly hearts that has been reawakened by this contact with the Bride and her tales of the Beloved?

The Bride's reply (5:10–16)

For the moment the Bride, in her own enthusiasm for her Beloved, seems to take their questions at face value. She launches out into a glowing paeon of the appearance and qualities of the Beloved.

It is like balm to her heart to sing freely of his worth and his beauty. The song arises from her inmost heart. It flows on; a beautifully modulated paeon of sheer joy. While she truly rejoices in the Beloved, her choice of word and phrase help us to grasp that her time in the harem and in the company of the King has taught her the acceptable mode of expression in these circles. While she expresses herself about the Beloved in her own way, there are also strong overtones of the 'courtly style' used of her by King Solomon. Perhaps the Bride is astute enough to know that only if she clothes her praise of the Beloved in this way will she make any impression on the courtly ladies – the Daughters of Jerusalem – and so persuade them to help her in her search for the Beloved.

She begins to eulogise his general appearance, his complexion and stature:

> My Beloved's complexion
> is radiant and ruddy;
> my Beloved is like a banner unfurled
> in the midst of ten thousand! (5:10)

He could thus never be mistaken, so compelling is his presence, so radiant and warm. By using of him the figure of a banner unfurled she is subtly alluding to and recalling her formula in 2:4 when she had sung that *his* banner unfurled over her was love. His very presence was easily discerned among the multitude.

The Beloved was more than handsome and attractive; his physical form was superior to all others:

> His head is like finest gold;
> his locks are wavy,
> and black as a raven.
> His eyes are pleasingly placed,
> like doves washed with milk
> beside the water brooks.
> His cheeks are like spices,
> like banks of aromatic herbs;
> his lips are like lilies
> distilling liquid myrrh. (5:11–13)

Her efforts to praise her Beloved in the style of the Court is only partially successful. The comparison with 'finest gold' used of his head, she would have learnt only recently. For the first time in her rustic life she had actually experienced the smooth glowing quality of real gold. Such an image would previously have been beyond her.

She cannot however sustain the court imagery for his other facial attributes. She naturally falls back on the long-familiar images of birds and plants. The black ravens of the country fields and woods, the blue-grey doves sitting peacefully in pairs at the brooks when she went to water her small flock: these are everyday realities. The spices, lilies and aromatic herbs of her garden: these images she happily transposes into a glowing description of the one whom her soul so loves.

As she proceeds, she becomes more adept at drawing

on her recent experiences of luxury in the King's dwelling, experiences with which the Daughters of Jerusalem were very familiar and for which they would have greater appreciation. Her awe at the grandeur of the cedars of Lebanon is also drawn into this verbal portrait of her Beloved:

> His hands are like circlets of gold
> embedded with beryl;
> overlaid with sapphires
> his torso is ivory
> polished and smooth.
> His limbs are columns of marble
> set upon sockets of finest gold;
> and his bearing is like Lebanon,
> stately as its cedars. (5:14,15)

Although the Bride uses her new-found knowledge of opulence and luxury in praise of the physique of her Beloved, there is nothing objectionably sensuous in her description – as there had been in King Solomon's appraisal of herself. Her song has the air of innocent and wholesome admiration. It conveys the nobility and loftiness of her most profound sentiments towards her Beloved. Hers is a song as opposite to and as exalted above the sentiments expressed by King Solomon as anything could be. As the Bride sings, a new world continues to open before the Daughters of Jerusalem. Long accustomed to worldly, sensual and ambitious words, they now listen intently as this simple country maid sings on about her Beloved:

> His speech is gracious,
> and he is wholly desirable.
> This is my Beloved,
> and this is my lover.
> O ye Daughters of Jerusalem! (5:16)

The curiosity of the Daughters of Jerusalem (6:1)

As she concludes, their admiration for her seems genuine. How had this simple, unlettered country girl learnt such beauty, such depth and purity of expression? Perhaps it was that reality she called love, which had taught her such wisdom; that love of which they knew so little in their world of sensuality and ambition and luxury.

For one brief moment they seem convinced, impressed and transported, as they in their turn ask the Bride:

> Whither has he gone, your Beloved,
> O fairest of women?
> Whither has your Beloved turned aside?
> That with you we may search for him! (6:1)

The Bride's jealousy (6:2–3)

There is something in their questioning and in their tone as they offer their services that gives the Bride cause to pause. Has she been too bold in praising the Beloved with such unreserved simplicity and spontaneity? Are these worldly women now rather too eager to seek him out for their own purposes rather than for hers?

The prick of something like nascent jealousy pierces the Bride's heart at their ardent words. Jealousy is a passion from which all who love deeply sooner or later suffer. This is the Bride's first taste, and it is bitter. It warns her that she is not as secure as she had presumed, in her relationship with her Beloved. She is captive and he is free. Now she has foolishly awakened a strong desire in these worldly women, and they evince too strong an interest in him. She is now fully awake to this new danger within her situation. Inwardly she resolves more determinedly than ever to find a way to escape from the harem as soon as possible.

Intuitively she changes her tactics with the Daughters of Jerusalem. She does this to safeguard her Beloved, to protect herself and to shield the integrity of their mutual love. She responds enigmatically to the women, in order to distract them from their intention to search for her Beloved:

> My Beloved is gone
> down into his garden,
> unto the banks of spices;
> gleaning the lilies,
> in the gardens taking his delight. (6:2)

After all, she tells them, I really do know where he has gone. I also know the way there. There is no need for you to go in search of him.

She emphatically lets them know that the relationship between herself and her Beloved is one of the most intimate mutuality, into which no one else can ever have the right to intrude.

> My Beloved is mine,
> and I am his:
> among the lilies
> he takes his delight! (6:3)

Yes, the Bride, and the Bride alone, is the garden of the Beloved.

In the Bride's heart, the scene is now set for her definitive escape from King Solomon. Recent events – his attempted farcical marriage with her, the ensuing panic and swoon in which she heard her Beloved urging her to take the initiative and escape from the oppressive domination of the King: these have moved her forward to her present conclusion that she needs to act promptly. In addition, her shattering, disturbing dream has unveiled her gradual accommodation to the material comforts of harem life, indicating her own lack of self-vigilance. Finally there are the stealthy stabs of jealousy over the attitude of the Daughters of Jerusalem to her Beloved. All these have sharpened to a fine point her determination to do the impossible, and escape from the clutches of the King.

The most powerful inducement propelling her towards a conclusive decision is the agonising memory of the departure of her Beloved in the dream. Even if it kills her, she absolutely must respond totally to his love and she must therefore find a way to evade the domination of the King.

The Bride has matured through all these experiences and through her increasingly responsible attitudes. These events have contributed to bring her to the point of being able to choose with determination and fortitude to elude the clutches of the King at any cost.

Finally she knows clearly what she should do, and how to do it. She only needs to await the desired moment which will unite her definitively with her Beloved.

*   *   *

The Bride needs the experience of shock to awaken her to her own shortcomings: some unexpected reversal of fortune in the daily routine, or some profoundly disturbing dream or mysterious visitation of the Beloved that does not go according to accustomed pattern. This kind of experience is imperative for a true 'second' conversion to the exigencies of eternal love which is the essential ingredient in the 'breakthrough' into freedom of life and union with the Beloved. But it is a conversion which the Beloved himself brings about by his mysterious and hidden action which always needs the reawakening and free consent of the Bride.

The Fifth Song of the Bride

KING SOLOMON *(to the Bride)*

6:4   You, my love,
                arc fair like Tirzah,
                beautiful like Jerusalem,
                terrible as an army
                with banners unfurled!

6:5   Turn away your eyes
                for they oppose me,
                because they slay me!

                Your hair is like
                a flock of goats
                gleaming on Gilead.

6:6   Your teeth are like
                a flock of ewes,
                coming from the sheep-dip,
                none of them on her own,
                and all of them
                perfectly paired.

6:7   Like a pomegranate cut in half
                are your cheeks
                behind your veil!

6:8   There are three-score queens,
                there are four-score concubines,
                and maidens without number,

6:9   but my perfect one,
                my dove, is unique;
                she is her mother's only one,

the chosen one,
of her who gave her birth!

The Daughters beheld her,
and they called her blessed!
the queens and the concubines
also saw her,
and they gave her praise:

DAUGHTERS, QUEENS AND CONCUBINES *(praising
the Bride)*
6:10   Who is this
arising like the dawn?
Fair as the moon?
Bright as the sun?
Terrible as an army
with banners unfurled!

BRIDE   *(recounting the story of her abduction and plainly
accusing King Solomon to his face)*
6:11   I had gone down
to the orchard of nuts,
to look at the herbs of the valley,
to see if the vines
had opened their buds,
to see if the promegranate trees
were in bloom;
6:12   when, (O my soul),
before I was aware,
YOU had placed me
upon the chariots of 'Aminadab'!

KING SOLOMON, DAUGHTERS, QUEENS AND
CONCUBINES IN CHORUS
*(summoning the dancing Bride to return back
along the double-filed assembly)*

7:1a   Return! Return!
          O Shulamitess!
          Return! Return!
          That we may behold you!

BRIDE   *(to King Solomon telling him that this dance is*
          the only thing that she is prepared to give him,
          nothing more)
7:1b   What will you see
          in the Shulamitess,
          but the dance
          of the double-file troop?!

KING SOLOMON: *(realising that he is making no head-*
          way with her makes one last impassioned bid for
          her consent)
7:2   How lovely are your sandalled steps,
          O daughter of the Prince!
          The joints of your thighs
          like the links of a chain,
          of the craftsman's art!
7:3   Your navel is a rounded bowl,
          lacking not mingled wine;
          your belly's like heaped up wheat
          encircled with lilies!

7:4   Your two breasts
          are like two fawns,
          the twins of a gazelle!
7:5   Your neck is like an ivory tower,
          your eyes like the pools of Heshbon
          close to the Gate of Beth-Rabbim,
          your nose, like the tower of Lebanon
          looking to Damascus!
7:6   Your head is like Carmel,
          and the hair of your head

like precious purple;
the King is held captive
in the tresses!

7:7   How lovely and how fair you are
for pleasure, O love!

7:8   You are stately like the palm-tree,
and your breasts
are like clusters of dates.

7:9   I will climb up the palm-tree,
I will grasp its fronds;
now let your breasts
be as the clusters of the vine,
and like apples
the fragrance of your breath.

7:10a   Your speech is like mellow wine . . .
*(At this moment the dancing Bride dances out
of the double-file into the surrounding darkness
and is swallowed up in the shadows where she
continues singing in exultant joy now that she is
free in the company of her waiting Beloved)*

BRIDE   *(taking up the very words of King Solomon and
giving them a different application)*

7:10b   . . . mellow wine
flowing softly on lips that slumber,
flowing straight to my Beloved!

7:11   I belong to my Beloved,
and his desire is for me!
*(At this point the meeting of the two Lovers
takes place)*

7:12   O come, my Beloved!
Let us go forth to the fields!
And in the hamlets let us lodge!

7:13   Let us rise early,
and go to the vineyards,

to see if the vine
has opened its buds,
and whether the grapes
have set in the blossom,
and if there are flowers
on the pomegranate trees!
There I will give you my love!

7:14   The mandrakes exhale their fragrance,
and over our doors
are all the choice fruits,
fresh fruit and dried,
which I have stored up
my Beloved, for you!

8:1   O, that you were
my very own brother,
who had been nursed
at my own mother's breast;
I could find you outside
and kiss you and not be despised!

8:2   I would lead you
and make you come
into my mother's own house,
that you would instruct me;
I would give you to drink spiced wine
of my pomegranate juice.

8:3   O that his left hand
were under my head,
and his right hand embracing me!

BRIDE   *(calling once more on the Daughters of Jerusalem
to show them how futile had been their efforts to
coerce love to awake)*

8:4   I adjure you, O Daughters of Jerusalem!
How can you arouse, and how awaken love,

until it pleases to awake?

CHORUS *(describing the Bride and her Beloved coming
        through the desert)*
8:5   Who is this,
        coming up from the desert,
        leaning upon her Beloved?

BELOVED *(to his Bride)*
        It was underneath the apple tree
        that I awakened you to love:
        there your mother
        was in travail with you,
        there she was in travail
        and gave you birth.

8:6   Set me as a seal upon your heart!

BRIDE   *(to her Beloved)*
        Set me as a seal upon your arm!

BRIDE AND BELOVED IN CHORUS
        *(proclaiming the praises and qualities of true and
        enduring love)*
        For love is as strong as death,
        and desire as unyielding as sheol.
        Its flames are the flames of fire,
        the very Flame of the Lord himself!

8:7   Many waters cannot quench love,
        nor swallow it up!
        Neither can the floods
        sweep it away!

        If a man gave for love
        all the wealth of his house,
        he would count it entirely as nought!

The Fifth Song of the Bride (6:4–8:7)

Prologue

Bride:

> O, that he would kiss me
> with the kisses of his mouth!
>
> 'More delightful than wine is your love!
> Delightful, the fragrance of your perfume!'
>
> Your name is perfume poured out!
> That is why the maidens love you!
> Draw me after you!
> Let us make haste!
> The King has forced me
> into his rooms! (1:1–4)

As a prologue to the fifth and final song of the Bride in Love's Fugue, the lines that stand out with special urgency are:

> Draw me after you!
> Let us make haste!

The Bride's resolve is firm. She is about to make her escape from the cruel dominion of the King, the prince of darkness and seduction. Hence she cries out interiorly with greater ardour than ever to her Beloved, depending on the power and strength of his love to help her remain sufficiently bold and daring to make good her escape against such odds. There is urgency: she feels time is running out – 'Let us make haste!'

*   *   *

The fifth and final song in Love's Fugue is the longest and most intricate and complex in its movements. The dramatic crisis of the Bride is resolved. The song moves through many dramatic movements until the Finale of the drama draws it to a close like a solemn cantata into which the fugue has melted. Interwoven with each dramatic movement there is a chorus which adds colour and heightened interest to this fascinating conclusion.

Altogether there are eleven elements closely inter-woven to make up the fabric of this moving song with its grand final chorus of love. Let us look briefly at the structure. There are two complementary main movements which unite the eleven lesser movements into one whole. The first movement can be entitled 'The flight of the Bride from the King'. The second movement: 'The flight of the Bride to and with the Beloved':

1. The flight of the Bride from the King (6:4–7:10a)
    (a) the overture of King Solomon (6:4–9)
    (b) the chorus of the Daughters, queens and concu-
        bines (6:10)
    (c) the confession of the Bride (6:11,12)
    (d) the chorus of the King, Daughters, queens and
        concubines (7:1a)
    (e) the challenge of the Bride (7:1b)
    (f) the final song of the King (7:2–10a).
2. The flight of the Bride to and with the Beloved
(7:10b–8:7)
    (a) the song of the Bride (7:10b–8:4)

(b) the chorus of the bystanders (8:5)
(c) the interlude of the Beloved (8:5b–6a)
(d) the Bride's response (8:6b)
(e) the chorus of the Bride and the Beloved (8:6b–7).

The flight of the Bride from the King (6:4–7:10a)

The setting of the first movement of the Fifth Song is a continuation of the mock wedding scene of the Third Song. In the interval between that abortive attempt at the ritual of the wasf the King has prepared himself with his full cast of Daughters of Jerusalem, queens, concubines and armed mighty men, to ensure that nothing goes awry in this celebration. The entire movement proceeds in dramatic stages to the climax of the sword-dance which was the characteristic feature of the wasf.

The assembly are gathered in the evening for the outdoor 'sword-dance' ceremony in which the chosen 'bride-to-be' is to dance the sword-dance between the double file of mighty men holding their swords over her. This ceremony took place traditionally on the night preceding the wedding night and at it the bridegroom sings the praise of the bride and her physical charms for all the company to hear and admire. In this song, King Solomon arrogantly, blatantly and deceitfully uses this ancient oriental custom to inveigle yet another young woman into a sham wedding with himself. In this case he has met his match in the simple Shulamitess.

The overture of King Solomon (6:4–9)
King Solomon's opening lines betray that he now sees something new and formidable in the simple Shulamitess: something before which he quakes and is inwardly shaken. However, in his habitual arrogance and suavity he attempts to clothe this startling new perception of her in phrases that

partially obscure this new knowledge from the unskilled and inattentive ear. To those present his words will sound like the old, familiar flattery:

> You, my love,
> are fair like Tirzah,
> beautiful like Jerusalem,
> terrible as an army
> with banner unfurled!
>
> Turn away your eyes
> for they oppose me,
> because they slay me! (6:4–5)

The Bride's newly acquired strength and self-assurance since their last encounter disturb the King. In their previous encounter he had been the presumptuous royal one: the superior, power person, surrounded by his three-score armed men, ready to conquer with ease this inexperienced, simple but extraordinarily beautiful country maid. But now he acknowledges her regal qualities by likening her beauty to the royal cities of Tirzah and Jerusalem. His armed strength – sixty fighting men girded with swords (3:8) – compares badly with the terrible strength of an army marching out to war with banners unfurled in the wind. This is what he now sees in the Shulamitess splendidly arrayed in the garments he has provided for the performance of the sword-dance on this very night.

He senses even worse danger to himself when he gazes into her eyes which twice before he has likened to the innocence and gentleness of doves:

> Behold, my love,
> your eyes are doves! (1:15; 4:1)

The eyes of the Shulamitess flash with a very different

light now – they haughtily oppose him and flash with a power that slays him.

The positions of Solomon and the Shulamitess are being subtly reversed. He is no longer so sure that he can lustfully dominate her and make her yield to his will. But old habits die hard. Once more he gathers together his seductive energies and sense of purpose. He returns to the attack. His first step is to repeat his former flattery in order to reassert his position of power over her:

> Your hair is like
> a flock of goats
> gleaming on Gilead.
> Your teeth are like
> a flock of ewes,
> coming from the sheep-dip,
> none of them on her own,
> and all of them
> perfectly paired.
> Like a pomegranate cut in half
> are your cheeks
> behind your veil! (6:5b–7)

His repeat performance of 4:1b,2,3 has little effect on the Shulamitess. She remains steadfast in her initial attitude of aloofness and antagonism to him. There seems to be no chink in her armour.

The King then resorts to a new tactic. If she will not yield to direct flattery, surely she, like every woman, will be impressed by a comparison of herself to other really beautiful women – such as his own hand-picked and prized selections of queens, concubines and maidens:

> There are three-score queens,
> there are four-score concubines,
> and maidens without number,

> but my perfect one,
> my dove, is unique;
> she is her mother's only one,
> the chosen one,
> of her who gave her birth! (6:8–9a)

The King's transition from direct address to the use of the third person, in referring to the Shulamitess, indicates that he is trying subtly to arouse her interest in himself. In his supposed infatuation with her beauty, he proclaims her loveliness in exuberant terms to those gathered for the sword-dance ceremony. If the assembly is impressed, she apparently is not.

So the King pursues his strategy by doing what his long experience has taught him no woman can resist. He boldly announces the infallible criterion of her beauty and desirability – other women, other very beautiful women have sung her praises! So he, after all, is only seeing and proclaiming what the very best women have seen and praised in her. Surely she will not refuse to yield before such powerful flattery:

> The Daughters beheld her,
> and they called her blessed!
> the queens and the concubines
> also saw her,
> and they gave her praise! (6:9b)

The chorus of the Daughters, queens and concubines (6:10)

As if to confirm the King beyond a shadow of doubt, the Daughters of Jerusalem, the three-score queens, and the four-score concubines of his harem break forth in the well-rehearsed and somewhat awesome chorus in praise of the lone Shulamitess:

> Who is this
> arising like the dawn?
> Fair as the moon?
> Bright as the sun?
> Terrible as an army
> with banners unfurled! (6:10)

It is a splendid, high feminine tribute to the beauty and solitary power of this simple Shulamitess. Any lesser person would have been impressed, flattered and won over by such glorious tribute paid so dramatically by other women in a united chorus.

If the King felt he had played his trump card, and was about to witness the capitulation of the Maid of Shulam, he was to be deeply disappointed and find himself grossly mistaken.

The confession of the Bride (6:11,12)

Into the expectant silence, with all eyes fastened on her solitary figure, the Shulamitess proceeds to proclaim in song, not the anticipated surrender to Solomon, but a bold confession of facts. She sings a clear, bold proclamation in yet more forthright terms; that her presence here in this assembly is neither of her own doing nor at all to her liking. She accuses and challenges to his face the royal abductor and seducer, so that all can hear.

It is a simple story. She had been going about her usual daily chores in the orchards and vineyards at the behest of her elder brothers, when the King's men, or the King himself, had arrived on the scene, snatching her away, ruthlessly oppressing her:

> I had gone down
> to the orchards of nuts,
> to look at the herbs of the valley,
> to see if the vines

had opened their buds,
to see if the pomegranate trees
were in bloom;
when, (O my soul),
before I was aware,
YOU had placed me
upon the chariots of 'Aminadab'. (6:11–12)

Thus she declares that the King himself had snatched her away unwillingly from her own people and place. He had forced upon her an abhorrent yoke of oppression among the princely people of his court. She is a stranger and foreigner in this setting, and always will be. Kingly and courtly ways with their worldliness, ambition and lust for power and pleasure, hold no attraction for her. It is useless for the King to oppress her, and even more futile to flatter her. No matter what tactic he uses to dominate her, he will never· be able to force her to change.

The chorus of the King, Daughters, queens and concubines (7:1a)

The more emphatically the Shulamitess protests, challenges and reproaches the King and his court for their corrupt ways, the more frenzied becomes their fascination with this simple country girl. Their chorus presses in around the Shulamitess (perhaps more wine than usual has flowed already at this gathering). Singing, they summon the dancing Shulamitess to return back along the double-filed ranks of the mighty men.

Return! Return!
O Shulamitess!
Return! Return!
That we may behold you! (7:1a)

The blood of the assembly is up. Things are maybe getting

a little out of hand. They want more of the Shulamitess and her dancing. They clamour for her to return yet again along the double file of armed men, in the manner of the dance. Perhaps, too, they are awakening to the fact that her words were telling them that she is already far removed from their world.

Bowing to the will and desire of their king and lord, as is their wont, they join with him to demand her return. They must turn her into one of themselves. Now that she is in their power, they must not let her go. By sheer weight of numbers they believe that they can bring her down. But perhaps too, their besotted minds are held captive by a strange curiosity about her – she is so different from themselves. Why?

The challenge of the Bride (7:1b)

The Shulamitess, fully in command of herself, flings her response at them in the form of a challenge. She tells the King above all, that this sword-dance is certainly *not* a prelude to any wedding as far as she is concerned, sham or otherwise. This dance is the only thing he will have from her: his last and only opportunity to witness her skill in dancing. That is all she is prepared to give him.

> What will you see
> in the Shulamitess,
> but the dance
> of the double-file troop?! (7:1b)

Her challenge flung at the King, the Shulamitess quickens the pace in her dance. She is the only one in the whole company without wine in her veins; hers is the only cool head in the entire assembly. She continues to mesmerise King Solomon and his cohort with the intricate skill of her dancing.

She knows that the moment of her escape is drawing near. The nature of this particular ceremony caused it to turn rapidly into an orgy, and already over-much wine has been shared. Instinctively too she knows that the visitation of her Beloved in her recent dreams is, in reality, scheduled for this particular night. She must not, will not, let him pass her by. She must be ready, alert, vigilant for that moment when he comes.

But the thoughts and intentions of the dancing maid are very different from those of the King who has never before in his lustful life been outwitted by a slip of a girl.

The final song of the King (7:2–10a)

The dancing girl mesmerises, fascinates the King, now heady with strong wine. Her dancing is indeed skilled beyond any dancing he has witnessed. He must not let her out of his power. She is too ripe for pleasure. Besides, she is his captive, his possession, as so many others have been before. So he raises his voice once more in sonorous, seductive strains, reaching out to her on the level most familiar to him – the seductive and the sensual.

He cannot know, so inured is he to deceit and domination, that his incantation of her physical charms will leave the Shulamitess unmoved. He is ignorant of the goal and values that draw and attract her so powerfully. As he watches her dancing, coolly aloof, her resolve elsewhere, the King sings the only kind of song he knows. That it will be in vain is lost on him:

> How lovely are your sandalled steps,
> O daughter of the Prince!
> The joints of your thighs
> like the links of a chain,
> of the craftsman's art!
> Your navel is a rounded bowl,

lacking not mingled wine;
your belly's like heaped up wheat
encircled with lilies! (7:2,3)

The physical details of his flattery go far beyond all his
previous remarks. For him, nothing in the Shulamitess
is sacred. In his description of her there is no vestige
of any attempt at propriety. She is for him merely a
bodily presence, an object of his lustful passions; if she
has not responded to him on that level, then he will
continue until she does. He knows no other logic. He
uses images and figures which are seemingly graceful
and lovely, but their meaning and content are entirely
sensuous:

Your two breasts
are like two fawns,
the twins of a gazelle!
Your neck is like an ivory tower,
your eyes like the pools of Heshbon
close to the Gate of Beth-Rabbim,
your nose, like the tower of Lebanon
looking to Damascus!
Your head is like Carmel,
and the hair of your head
like precious purple;
the King is held captive
in the tresses! (7:4–6)

Does he seek to impress her by comparing her physical
make-up to the various places of beauty and prominence
in his territory? Does he really find her bodily person as
rich and varied as implied in these comparisons – the
grace of gazelles, the verdure and reservoirs of Heshbon,
or the chief place of assembly in a populous city; the

regal aspect of Lebanon's tower, the solitary majesty of Carmel, and the desired and sought-after purple dye? And can he, the deceiver, be believed when he claims that he is held captive in her tresses, the traditional 'net of love'?

His sincerity is readily cast into doubt by the following verses. These seem to confirm that he is firmly convinced that every woman will ultimately succumb to temptation provided it is persistently presented in sufficiently sensuous terms.

So he proceeds, sure now of conquest and domination, and revealing that it is mere pleasure he seeks, rather than love. His lying wiles show no concern for the person and dignity of the Bride, but only his search for gratification of his own insatiable lust which ever seeks to grasp and plunder pleasure where he desires it:

> How lovely and how fair you are
> for pleasure, O love!
> You are stately like the palm-tree,
> and your breasts
> are like clusters of dates.
> I will climb up the palm-tree,
> I will grasp its fronds;
> now let your breasts
> be as the clusters of the vine,
> and like apples
> the fragrance of your breath.
> Your speech is like mellow wine . . . (7:7–10a)

The lust for power, possession and pleasure inevitably overreaches itself if left long enough to run its self-destructive course. As the King sings on in his lustful serenade we leave him, perhaps with the cup of wine in his hand. From this point in the song we follow the Bride.

By what is perhaps an odd coincidence, the text is broken and interrupted at this point.

The flight of the Bride to and with the Beloved (7:10b–8:7)

At the point of the break in the text, the Bride also discerns a break in the vigilance of the sword-armed double-file troop. Perhaps it is a slackness from weariness or drunkenness at the end of the line where the revelry of the King merges into the darkness of the night. As she dances, the Bride slips through this gap with cool boldness and is swallowed up into the night. She does not return or continue her dance for the King.

As she takes up the broken melody of the King's text, she transforms it into a new modality. Gone is the milieu of the King's world of lust, sensuality and pleasure for pleasure's sake, and domination of the weak by the strong. Vanished is the spirit of plunder, tyranny, sensual ambition and egoism.

The song of the Bride (7:10b–8:4)
From now on, with the change of scene, the world of lust and King Solomon retreats and fades away as the world of integrity in love emerges with ever more confidence. The non-relationship of Solomon to the Bride is replaced by the true relationship of the Beloved to her in love's mutual and freely given response, in a spirit of reverence and shared gift.

Once the comforting darkness of the night has enveloped the Bride as she dances out of the long line of the 'double-filed troop', she knows with certainty that her Beloved is there in the velvety blackness, waiting for her, drawing her urgently after him, saying as in the original Prologue: 'Let us make haste!' (1:4).

So, in a completely new modality the Bride takes up the Song of Love, transforming the final words of Solomon's:

> . . . mellow wine
> flowing softly on lips that slumber,
> flowing straight to my Beloved!
>
> I belong to my Beloved,
> and his desire is for me! (7:10b–11)

These are the transitional verses. The world of King Solomon's revelry recedes. The relationship of love between the reunited Bride and her Beloved unfolds before our eyes.

The Bride subtly likens the gentle flowing movement of wine on slumbering lips to the contentment of true love. She has been in some kind of slumber or torpor during her cruel captivity, but she has now awakened in real earnest. Her love is the mellow wine savoured by her Beloved:

> More delightful than wine is your love! (1:2b)
> How delightful your love,
> more delightful than wine,
> my Sister, my Bride! (4:9)

She tells the Beloved that now, without reserve, and by her free and responsible choice, she is flowing straight towards him, even as she knows that he too is overflowing in *his desire for her*. Now that she has achieved her escape from the clutches of the King she is definitively liberated to flow towards, to be united to the Beloved.

Thus the Bride/wine flowing out to her Beloved meets the Beloved coming to her overflowing with desire. This is perhaps the only time in the entire scriptures that we meet this phrase which is the complete reversal of Genesis

3:16 where God told the woman that her desire, longing, yearning, would be for her husband. Here in this verse of the Song it is the Beloved who is the one drawn by deep desire to and for his Bride. There is much to ponder here. In the enfolding mantle of the night the Bride and the Beloved meet and continue their flight of love together.

The Bride's song flows on predictably, inviting her Beloved to come with her back to the earlier scenes where he had first awakened her love for him: to the fields, the vineyards and the garden where the drama of love had begun.

In all the harsh days of her captivity her Beloved had secretly 'lodged in her bosom, her heart like a bundle of myrrh' (1:13): the perfume of his memory comforting and encouraging her in her tribulations. Now she is free again they can both 'lodge' in the hamlet familiar to them.

Together they can go in the dawn hours to revisit the vineyards, gardens, the pomegranate trees in bloom, just as she had done alone on that fateful morning when she had been seized and snatched away into captivity by King Solomon (1:6; 6:11,12). Now there will be no danger, for she and her Beloved can go together and share the delights of the nut orchard, the vineyard and the garden – yes, even her very own garden. Then all that she has dreamed about in her captivity will be enjoyed with her Beloved (2:10–14; 4:6–12; 5:1; 6:2–3).

Rejoicing now in her new-found freedom and maturity in love, she sings gladly inviting her Beloved:

> O come, my Beloved!
> Let us go forth to the fields!
> And in the hamlets let us lodge!
> Let us rise early,
> and go to the vineyards,
> to see if the vine

> has opened its buds,
> and whether the grapes
> have set in the blossom,
> and if there are flowers
> on the pomegranate trees!
> There I will give you my love! (7:12–13)

While the Bride sings, it becomes clear that the time is ripe for the formal, mutual sealing of their love. As part of her movement towards this full union she proceeds to spell out some of her personal preparation for this moment. Her Beloved had earlier, in her dream, spoken of his desire to come into his garden (his Bride) and to delight in the fruits thereof (2:13; 4:12–14; 4:16). And to this she had already invited him – but this song is her full and final invitation (a year may have passed since her abduction).

She tells him that now is the time of the mandrakes, the apples of the Mandragora, the ancient plant symbolising love and fecundity. This she is now ready to offer him, together with all the other fruits of love, fresh and dried, which she has carefully selected and stored up for him, and him alone, in her life and person. Her song flows on:

> The mandrakes exhale their fragrance,
> and over our doors
> are all the choice fruits,
> fresh fruit and dried,
> which I have stored up
> my Beloved, for you! (7:14)

As the Song of the Bride flows on, it inevitably returns to the question of the 'brothers' and the mother of the Bride. She has now reached maturity in love and is competent to deal with that vexatious topic: the elder brothers who had been the cause of so much pain and trouble to her at the beginning of the story. Her mother, too, will now need to accept the Bride's Beloved and the permanent nature of their mutual love. The Beloved will now need to find a welcome within the family circle.

The Bride now can no longer tolerate any secretiveness about their relationship, which is honourable, noble and praiseworthy. She will have to arrange for him to come right into the family circle and take his rightful place and continue to teach her – and her mother and brothers – the further and deeper lessons of love which he alone is competent to impart.

The Bride will tend his needs and regale him with the delicacies and spiced wine which she has prepared for him from her own garden. All these concepts are contained in the next verses of her song:

> O, that you were
> my very own brother,
> who had been nursed
> at my own mother's breast;
> I could find you outside
> and kiss you and not be despised!
> I would lead you
> and make you come
> into my mother's own house,
> that you would instruct me;
> I would give you to drink spiced wine
> of my pomegranate juice. (8:1–2)

She concludes this part of her song by returning to the expression she had earlier used to describe her desire and yearning for intimacy between herself and her Beloved as she had sung of it in 2:6:

> O that his left hand
> were under my head,
> and his right hand embracing me! (8:3)

As she and her Beloved continue their journey to the
hamlets under cover of the night, she continues to sing to
him of her story during her time in King Solomon's harem.
At this point she now muses back to her oft-repeated
questioning of the Daughters of Jerusalem about their
persistent attempts to forcibly arouse and awaken in
her some kind of love for King Solomon, the seducer.
She sings again her chorus to them, for her Beloved to
hear, asking it now more as a kind of rhetorical question
to anyone who may be interested in the genesis of love:

> I adjure you, O Daughters of Jerusalem!
> How can you arouse, and how awaken love,
> until it pleases to awake? (8:4)

She is stating that in the final analysis love is entirely
free. It can never be cajoled or coerced into wakefulness.
Force and coercion were the basic mistakes made by King
Solomon and his worldly-minded retinue. Love and lust
belong to two entirely different orders of reality. They
cannot and may not be mixed together, any more than
oil and water.

The progress of the Bride and Beloved through the
desert night to the old familiar hamlet is drawing to its
close just as the dawn begins to break. It is fitting now
that a new chorus of new bystanders sing out and rejoice
in their coming.

The chorus of bystanders (8:5)
This is very different from the two earlier choruses of
bystanders. It does not proclaim any such empty pomp as
the chorus in 3:6 which announced the ornate, luxurious,
splendid procession of King Solomon as he advanced to
his attempted mock marriage with the Shulamitess. Nor
does it possess the dramatic clarity and intensity of the

chorus of the Daughters, queens and concubines praising the appearance of the Bride as she enters into the critical episode of the sword-dance in 6:10.

This chorus is devoid of all such worldly, superficial and shallow glitter. There is no fanfare heralding the dramatic exploits of the courageous Bride. There is no noisy acclamation of her courage and endurance while she was on trial for love. All that we hear is a simple, almost homely, statement of fact: a discreet portrayal of the Bride and her Beloved coming up from the silence and darkness of places and experiences which are significantly designated under one word: the desert. What has transpired in the dark, dangerous desert receives no mention – that is no longer necessary. The reality that grows ever brighter with the receding night and emerging dawn is the reality of integrity in love.

The chorus is short, opens quietly, and is gone almost before we have caught the full import of its message:

> Who is this,
> coming up from the desert,
> leaning upon her Beloved? (8:5)

No reply need be given to this chorus. The Bride and her Beloved have returned home openly; that is enough. Everyone should be satisfied and well content.

The interlude of the Beloved (8:5b–6a)

The Beloved now raises his voice in song: one of the few occasions he has done so in the entire fugue. His role seems to have been rather one of influential absence than of provocative presence, but now he makes one of his most important statements. He declares that it was his own achievement and his sole right to awaken love in the breast of the Bride. He has done this not by any spectacular or dramatic scenario, such as was vainly attempted by the prince seducer, King Solomon. He has done it simply by going to the very apple tree in the garden which had seen the beginnings of the Bride's own life – her birthplace. In other words, he had encountered her with simplicity and sincerity, and reached out to her at the very root and origin of her personality. He had touched the inner core of her being. At his presence and at his touch she had awoken and responded with integrity and constancy in love. He, her only Beloved, could now claim her, publicly, as his own. He sings:

> It was underneath the apple tree
> that I awakened you to love:
> there your mother
> was in travail with you,
> there she was in travail
> and gave you birth.
> Set me as a seal upon your heart! (8:5b–6a)

The Bride's response (8:6)

> Set me as a seal upon your arm! (8:6)

In this way the Beloved and the Bride pledge their mutual love. The seal upon the heart and the seal upon the arm was an ancient expression and practice between those bound together by such intimate love, a prelude to their formal marriage ceremony.

The chorus of the Bride and the Beloved (8:6b–7)

After this mutual pledge of their love for each other using the symbols of the seal, the Bride and her Beloved now sing of the value and integrity of authentic love. This superb outburst of song is a magnificent canticle sung in perfect harmony.

The depth and divinity of love are proclaimed. They sing of its strength and endurance, its power and persuasion and ineffable value in images of superlative conviction. Never has the integrity of love been so extolled by human lips. As we listen to this compelling chorus we too are drawn in to the divine influence of love, held spellbound and convinced as the final cadences die away:

> For love is as strong as death,
> and desire as unyielding as sheol.
> Its flames are the flames of fire,
> the very Flame of the Lord himself!
>
> Many waters cannot quench love,
> nor swallow it up!
> Neither can the floods
> sweep it away!
>
> If a man gave for love
> all the wealth of his house,
> he would count it entirely as nought! (8:6b–7)

This is the Song of the Bride and the Beloved. It is the Song of Love. The story of the Bride has proved their chorus to be valid and true. For the sake of love, driven by desire, the Bride has passed through fire and through the waters of tribulation; she has surrendered everything she had, she was brought to the brink of choosing death rather than life for the sake of the integrity of love, and counted it all for nought.

The story of this Shulamitess, the maid from the country, teaches us that love alone can awaken love in the human heart; and love alone is a mysterious power purifying and perfecting the human heart through the choices it draws the person to make by quickening the undying desire for integrity in love.

It remains now to listen to the preparations for the marriage between the Bride and the Beloved in the Epilogue to Love's Fugue.

*   *   *

Thus ends the conflict between lust and love, the prince of darkness and the Beloved of eternal light. The final stanzas of the Spiritual Canticle of John of the Cross find their fullest interpretation in these concluding verses of the Fifth Song of Love's Fugue. The Bride flies with her Beloved in the serene night emerging into dawn, fleeing to the Garden of Delight, the flame and the water torrents that prove and test love's integrity. Here Aminadab cannot venture to come; he retreats, defeated, together with his cohort:

> The breathing of the air,
> the song of the sweet nightingale,
> the grove and its living beauty,
> in the serene night,
> with a flame that consumes and gives no pain.
> No one looked at it
> nor did Aminadab appear;
> the siege was still;
> and the cavalry,
> at the sight of the waters, descended – was defeated!

Epilogue

THE BRIDE'S BROTHERS *(laying down their conditions for endowing her in a rich manner on her wedding day)*

8:8 We have a young sister,
  with breasts still unformed;
  what shall we do for our sister,
  on the day wherein she shall be spoken for?

8:9 If she be a wall,
  upon her we will build
  bulwarks of silver;
  but if she be a door,
  we will board her up
  with panels of cedar!

BRIDE *(to her brothers, reassuring them)*
8:10 I am a wall,
  and my breasts are as towers,
  since I was in his presence
  as one finding peace!

BRIDE *(against King Solomon once more)*
8:11 Solomon had a vineyard,
  at Bayal Hamon;
  he let the vineyard out to keepers;
  a thousand pieces of silver,
  every man was to bring him for its fruit!

8:12 My vineyard, my very own,
  belongs to me!

You, Solomon, can have the thousand,
and the keepers of the fruit,
the two hundred!

BELOVED *(searching for his Bride)*
8:13   O you who dwell in the gardens,
the friends are listening
to your voice!
Let me hear your voice!

BRIDE   *(her final call and invitation to her Beloved)*
8:14   Make haste, my Beloved!
Be like a gazelle,
or like a young hart,
upon the mountains of spices!

Epilogue (8:8–14)

The Epilogue to the five songs of Love's Fugue is a record of the reminiscences of the Bride over the drama of her story and the way in which she remained steadfastly faithful to the integrity of her love for her Beloved. The content leads us to see and hear in this final movement the preparations for the approaching wedding day of the Bride and the Beloved.

The Epilogue opens with the elder brothers of the Bride stating their conditions regarding the marriage dowry they are prepared to provide for her. Then we hear the Bride's reassurance in the face of their anxiety over her having safeguarded her virginity. This is followed by the Bride's personal opinion of King Solomon and his corrupt ways.

There is finally the delicately worded dialogue between the Beloved and the Bride, couched in terms that flood our minds with the fine imagery of their earlier meeting in the five songs.

The brothers lay down their conditions for the bridal dowry (8:8–9)

The brothers make their offers of a generous dowry to their little sister on her future wedding day subject to the condition that when that day finally comes she can offer proofs of her virginity. If she has resisted all seductive temptations, remaining the strong wall of a fortress against every invader, they will endow her generously; but if she has become like an open door admitting any who would seduce her, and loses her virginity, then they will take measures to wall her up with strong planks for her own protection.

> We have a young sister,
> with breasts still unformed;
> what shall we do for our sister,
> on the day wherein she shall be spoken for?
>
> If she be a wall,
> upon her we will build
> bulwarks of silver;
> but if she be a door,
> we will board her up
> with panels of cedar! (8:8–9)

They make their offer very plainly against the 'day wherein she shall be spoken for' – that is, when the offer of marriage is made to or for her. This was their offer and their warning while she was still an immature adolescent girl.

The Bride, the one who used to be their 'little sister' makes reply.

The Bride reassures her brothers (8:10)

Now that she has passed unscathed through her terrible abduction by King Solomon with its searing trials, she is able to reply to her brothers in a way that completely satisfies their anxious and cautious brotherly hearts.

She confidently tells them that she is no longer their 'little sister'. By taking up their figure or image of a building, she lets them know that her 'breasts are as towers'; that is, she is now a mature woman. Moreover, she has safeguarded her virginity and is therefore not a 'door', but a 'wall'. Because of her single-minded love for her only Beloved, she has kept her virginal integrity and is at peace in the face of their conjectures.

> I am a wall,
> and my breasts are as towers,
> since I was in his presence
> as one finding peace! (8:10)

Her reply is a striking testimony to the enduring quality of integrity implanted in her by love rather than lust. She is no longer an unformed, immature girl; she is now a fully developed woman of proven virtue who has maintained the virginal integrity, fidelity and nobility of authentic love in the midst of lustful oppression and coercion on the part of the abductor King Solomon and those in his harem.

There is perhaps a two-edged thrust at King Solomon in her expression – 'since in his presence I was as one finding peace!' The very name Solomon means the 'peaceful one', and yet in her experience of him she found that with his lust for power, pleasure and possession he had betrayed in the deepest way the entire meaning of his name. Whereas she, the Shulamitess (which also means the 'peaceful one') had, by her uncluttered, simple integrity even in his lion's den of lust, been as one finding true peace through integrity and her fidelity to her true Beloved.

She continues to berate King Solomon's activities in the way he rented out his vineyard at Bayal Hamon.

The vineyard of King Solomon and the vineyard of the Bride (8:11–12)

> Solomon had a vineyard,
> at Bayal Hamon;
> he let the vineyard out to keepers;
> a thousand pieces of silver,
> every man was to bring him for its fruit! (8:11)

The very name of the place of Solomon's vineyard meant 'the master of a multitude' – a subtle reference to his harem and the multitude of his concubines, perhaps? At any rate he used it for a lucrative trade in order to increase his already surpassingly great wealth. In these words the Bride tells us of his nature not as a man of peace, but as a man who was avaricious and grasping for gain.

The term 'Bayal Hamon' also has resonances of continuous agitation and of murmuring or humming. So here again the Bride is continuing the idea that King Solomon, for all his wealth, power and lust, was not a man who was a master of peace. In fact she, the Shulamitess, who had all the odds stacked against her, has found the path to peace through love.

She returns here finally to tidy up the question of her former lack of vigilance over her own vineyard – her own person. She says:

> My vineyard, my very own,
> belongs to me!
>
> You, Solomon, can have the thousand,
> and the keepers of the fruit,
> the two hundred! (8:12)

Once more we see how astute is the Bride in her assessment of King Solomon; she has seen through his dealings with the keepers of his vineyard. The unfortunate keepers had to give him a thousand pieces of silver, while retaining only two hundred for themselves after their hard labour in the vineyard. You can have that if you like, she says, and the foolish keepers can have their pittance from you, hard taskmaster that you are. But I am more than content with my own vineyard. I could never consider being your chattel or one of your keepers.

She has learnt, to her cost, that vigilance over herself

and over her own poor vineyard is the only important thing in life. Such vigilance is the way to win love and to keep it, in the serenity of peace.

The final dialogue of the Beloved and the Bride (8:13–14)

The final garden scene and the snatch of conversation between the Beloved and the Bride are so full of delicate delight and sensitivity expressing the perfection of mutual contentment and trust in love's integrity that they need no comment.

> O you who dwell in the gardens,
> the friends are listening
> to your voice!
> Let me hear your voice! (8:13)

The Beloved is seeking her, his Bride, and knows now that she is to be found in her garden of delights, in the company of friends.

> Make haste, my Beloved!
> Be like a gazelle,
> or like a young hart,
> upon the mountains of spices! (8:14)

The many flights of love and love's desire are wrapped up in these final words of Love's Fugue. There is the Bride's flight of desire to be loved by the Beloved. There is the Beloved's flight of desire and love for the Bride. There is the mutual flight of Bride and Beloved to the place, and state, of their abiding rest, in the Garden of Delights!

Bibliography

Bernard of Clairvaux, *On the Song of Songs, Vols I, II, III, IV,* CF4; CF7; CF31; CF40, Cistercian Fathers Series (Kalamazoo: Cistercian Publications, 1976–1980).

Bernard of Clairvaux, *The Song of Songs,* ed. Halcyon Backhouse (London: Hodder and Stoughton, 1990).

Brown, Raymond E., S.S., *The Jerome Biblical Commentary* (London: Geoffrey Chapman, 1970). (Murphy, R.E., O. Carm., *Canticle of Canticles.*)

Cohen, Dr A., MA, Ph.D., D.H.L. (ed.), *The Five Megilloth,* Hebrew text and English translation with introductions and commentary (London, The Soncino Press, 1977, 13th impression).

Cohen, Dr A., *The Septuagint Version of the Old Testament and Apocrypha,* with an English translation by Sr Launcelot Lee Brenton (London: Samuel Bagster and Sons Ltd, 1976).

Cohen, Dr A., *Nova Vulgata Bibliorum Sacrorum,* Editio Sacros. Oecium. Concilii Vaticani II Ratione Habita Iussa Pauli PP. VI Recognita Auctoritate Ioannis Pauli PP. II Promulgata, Libreria Editrice Vaticana, 1979.

Dunstan, Ralph, Mus. Doc. Cantab., L. Mus. T.C.L., etc., *A Cyclopaedic Dictionary of Music* (London: J. Curwen & Sons Ltd, 1925, 4th ed.).

Elliger, K., et Rudolph, W. (Editio Funditu Renovata), *Biblia Hebraica Stuttgartensia* (Stuttgart: Deutsche Bibelgesellschaft, 1967/77).

Fuller, R. G. (gen. ed.), *A New Catholic Commentary on Holy Scripture* (London: Thomas Nelson & Sons Ltd,

1969). (Saydon, P.P., and Revd. Castellino, G., S.D.B., *The Song of Songs*.)

Gilbert of Hoyland (trans. Braceland, L. C., S.J.), *Sermons on the Song of Songs, I, II, III*, CF14; CF20; CF26, Cistercian Fathers Series (Kalamazoo, Cistercian Publications, 1978, 1979).

John of the Cross (ed. E. Allison Peers), *The Complete Works of Saint John of the Cross: Volume II Spiritual Canticle, Poems* (London: Burns Oates & Washbourne Ltd, 1934).

John of Ford (trans. Wendy Mary Beckett), *Sermons on the Final Verses of the Song of Songs, Vols I, II, III*, CF29; CF39; CF43, Cistercian Fathers Series (Kalamazoo: Cistercian Publications, 1977–1982).

Jones, A. (ed.), *The Jerusalem Bible* (London: Darton, Longman & Todd, 1966).

León-Dufour, Xavier (ed.), *Dictionary of Biblical Theology* (London: Geoffrey Chapman, 1978).

Lethielleux, M. P. (ed.), *Biblia Sacra* (Paris: Séminaire Saint-Sulpice, 1890).

Lethielleux, M. P., *La Sainte Bible* (traduite en francais sous la direction de L'École Biblique de Jérusalem), (Paris: Les Éditions du Cerf, 1956).

Luis de Léon, Fray, *La Perfecta Casada: Exposición del Cantar de Cantares, de Salomon* (Madrid: Aguilar, 1970).

McKenzie, John L., S.J., *Dictionary of the Bible* (London: Geoffrey Chapman, 1965).

Murphy, Roland E., *Book of Song of Songs*, Anchor Bible Dictionary, Vol. 6, pp. 150ff.

Orchard, Dom Bernard, MA (ed.), *A Catholic Commentary on Holy Scripture* (London: Thomas Nelson & Sons Ltd, 1957).

Origen, (trans. R. P. Lawson), *The Song of Songs*, commentary and homilies (London: The Newman Press, Longman's, Green and Co., 1957).

Pope, Marvin H., *Song of Songs*, The Anchor Bible (New York: Doubleday & Company Inc., 1977).

San Juan de la Cruz, *Poesía Completa* (Edición y notas – Jorge Garza Castillo), (Barcelona: Edicomunicación, S.A., 1992).

Snaith, Norman Henry, *Hebrew Old Testament* (London: The British & Foreign Bible Society, 1966, reprint).

Wansbrough, Henry, OSB, (gen. ed.), *The New Jerusalem Bible* (London: Darton, Longman & Todd, 1985).

Wansbrough, Henry, *Biblia de Jerusalén* (trans. dirigida por José A. Ubieta), (Bilbao, Desclee de Brouwer, 1975).